The Faith Factor
in Healing

The Faith Factor in Healing

THOMAS A. DROEGE

TRINITY PRESS INTERNATIONAL
Philadelphia

First Published 1991

Trinity Press International
3725 Chestnut Street
Philadelphia, PA 19104

Interior design and production by Publishers' WorkGroup
Cover design by Steven Zellers

Library of Congress Cataloging-in-Publication Data

Droege, Thomas A. (Thomas Arthur)
   The faith factor in healing / Thomas A. Droege.
      p.   cm.
   Includes bibliographical references and index.
   ISBN 1-56338-001-3
   1. Medicine—Religious aspects. 2. Spiritual healing. I. Title.
BL65.M4D76 1991
616.8'52—dc20   90-24688
                                                              CIP

CONTENTS

Foreword by William Foege   vii

Introduction   1

1. The Expanding Boundaries of Modern Medicine   6

2. The Placebo Effect—Faith Healing in Medicine   15

3. Framing Our Stories of Illness and Healing   34

4. The Use of Imagery in Healing   67

5. The Use of Imagery in the Church's Healing Ministry   94

FOREWORD

We live in the age of science and accept without amazement or bewilderment discoveries such as a new galaxy with billions of stars and a vaccine against Hepatitis B which, given early in life can prevent the development of liver cancer in middle age, thus becoming the first vaccine against cancer. We accept such break-throughs because we have been conditioned to believe that science will eventually not just let us know all, but that science will continue inexorably along a road that will develop the needed skills and knowledge to defeat disease.

Over thirty years ago, I was fascinated by a book on the great epidemics of history, written by Geddes Smith and entitled *Plague on Us*. The book took a certain pride in the role played by science in replacing the myths of the past with the truths of the present. But lest we become too proud, the final phrase in the epilogue provided a different perspective: "How much the men of science know about things they still do not understand." Now, in this book, Thomas Droege enters this world of plentiful knowledge and deficient understanding to ask where and how faith fits into the process of healing.

My first test in medical school was a time of stress, a time of memorizing facts, a time to focus with intensity on histology and a newly acquired knowledge of cells and their workings. It was surprising to the point of disorientation to enter the examination hall and be given a single question to write on for one hour: What is life? We approach a time when science's relentless quest to understand the universe and how it works will give way to the much more difficult task of understanding what it means. As Stephen Hawking reminds us, even if we understood the universe it would still be a set of rules and equations. Then, he says, we must ask, What is it that breathes fire into the equations and makes a universe for them to describe? Why does the universe go to all the bother of existing? Those of us interested in healing need a better understanding of what life is and what breathes fire into it, and a better understanding of the interactions of mind, body, and faith. Thomas Droege takes us on a tour of where some of our future efforts must be directed.

The changes in medicine have been frequently lauded. The changes in health are even more sensational. In my parents' lifetime, infant mortality in the United States has decreased from 150 deaths per 1000 live births to 10. Life expectancy at birth has increased by over twenty-five years. Now we are beginning to see the same revolution in developing countries. In the short span of thirty years, infant mortality rates have been cut in half in many countries, life expectancy at birth has reached sixty years, and children are now routinely protected against measles, polio, diphtheria, whooping cough, and tetanus. By the end of this century the life expectancy of the world's population will have increased to sixty-five, the once feared poliomyelitis will have disappeared, and children around the world will have a good chance of making it to adulthood. We now know that reducing infant and childhood deaths is a powerful ingredient in lowering birth rates and moving toward a solution to the population explosion. It is almost impossible to adequately express the profound change this has had and will continue to have on the quality of life.

And yet certain aspects of this change continue to haunt us. First, while we credit science with the advances, many of the improvements, such as the reduction of tuberculosis, began before scientific breakthroughs could have had an impact. Second, for almost every cause of death, the death rates are still higher for the lowest socioeconomic groups, even when scientists correct for everything known. Something accounts for this, but to date it eludes the best analysis of scientists. Could it be that poverty often engenders a fatalistic approach to life and this in turn influences some aspect of the body-mind communication discussed here by Thomas Droege?

Gandhi once said we should seek interdependence with the same diligence with which we seek self-sufficiency. We are increasingly heeding this wisdom as we recognize the implications for people of all cultures and for all future times of such problems as deforestation, the greenhouse effect, and acid rain. Thomas Droege provides here a roadmap to examine different aspects of this interdependence, such as the synergism of faith with other aspects of healing within an individual, the interdependence of healers and those being healed, and the interdependence of disciplines. Particularly intriguing is his depiction of physicians as "faith healers," a skill to be strengthened rather than denied. He also points out the dilemma of placebo studies, usually regarded as a comparison between an intervention and a placebo and therefore a straightforward, objective evaluation of the effect of a drug or other intervention on its own. In fact, as we learn, the placebo group provides a measure of the faith effect, the intervention group provides a measure of the intervention plus faith, and most studies provide no measure comparing the results to no intervention at all.

In 1989 the Institute of Medicine issued a research briefing titled *Behavioral Influences on the Endocrine and Immune Systems.* The briefing concluded, "The scientific data generally support the idea that the nervous system directly or through neuroendocrine mechanisms can affect the immune system." Yet the gaps in knowledge regarding mechanisms, relationships, and how to creatively use that knowledge remind us of "how much we know about the things we don't understand." Thomas Droege provides a stimulating account that broadens the understanding and awe of the healing process.

Finally, how fitting to dedicate this book to Wolfgang Bulle. Dr. Bulle has continued, over a remarkable career, to understand

the limitations of medicine or even science alone in addressing
the needs of people. His has been a career of both faith and
science.

William H. Foege, M.D.
Executive Director
The Carter Center
Atlanta, Georgia

INTRODUCTION

Health and spirituality, once regarded as the separate domains of medicine and religion, are currently regarded as complementary aspects of whole-person health care. Modern medicine is being nudged in the direction of including spirituality under health care by research studies that offer convincing evidence of body-mind communication. At no time in modern history has there been a greater opportunity for cooperation between religion and medicine in the promotion of health and healing.

The key term for making the connection between health and spirituality is faith. Put more precisely, there is a faith factor in healing. That will come as no surprise to those who are familiar with the history of healing in religion. It is prominent in the healing stories of Jesus, for example, when he tells the woman who touches his garment that her faith has made her well (Mark 5:34). But it is a surprise to have faith mentioned as a factor in medical healing. Herbert Benson of Harvard Medical School, well known for his promotion of the healing effects of the relaxation response, has recently identified a faith factor that further enhances the healing that comes with relaxation.[1]

Benson has spent a major part of his career studying the body's physiological response to relaxation, which can be measured by a decreased rate of breathing, lower blood pressure, a decreased heart rate, and slower brain waves. He contends that

1. Herbert Benson, *Beyond the Relaxation Response* (New York: Times Books, 1984).

the relaxation response counteracts the harmful effects and uncomfortable feelings of stress, which Hans Selye has identified as a factor in many diseases. Benson was one of the first to demonstrate that people can alter their body temperature and other physiological functions generally thought to be involuntary through practices such as meditation, imagery, and relaxation. Numerous studies, many of them using subjects who practice Transcendental Meditation, have demonstrated the effects of the relaxation response.

The instructions for inducing the relaxation response are simple: choose a comfortable position, close your eyes, relax your muscles, become aware of your breathing, maintain a passive attitude, and repeat a neutral word or sound. In *Beyond the Relaxation Response*, Benson states that he has "come to understand that the effects of this simple technique, *combined with a person's deepest personal beliefs*, can create other internal environments that can help the individual reach enhanced states of health and well-being."[2]

> The main idea is to develop a positive, powerful attitude, which provides us with a strong sense of control and equanimity, so that the best health we're capable of flows naturally from our brains to our bodies. The best combination to achieve this end seems to be a linkage between (1) a strong personal belief system, which encourages the possibility of achieving and maintaining good health; and (2) an enhancement of the healing power of this belief through the Relaxation Response. This combination is what I've called the Faith Factor.[3]

Repeating a brief phrase or word that reflects your belief system accomplishes two things. First, it activates the belief system and its accompanying benefits by providing a greater calming effect than might be achieved with a neutral focus word. Second, it increases the likelihood of using the technique. According to Benson, the conviction you have about the unique power of your faith plays a central role in what can be achieved with the faith factor. It is faith-in-general that he is talking about, the content of

2. Ibid., p. 5.
3. Ibid., pp. 85f.

2

the belief system being a factor only in that it has meaning to the person affirming it.

Benson's faith factor is a clear-cut example of a medical use of spirituality for the purpose of enhancing health and well-being. He is not promoting a particular religion, of course, but he is advocating a religious practice and doing it within an expanded view of medicine's role in promoting health. However one might evaluate his proposal, it serves as an excellent example of the relation between health and spirituality.

Not many medical authorities make specific reference to faith as a factor in healing, but there is a general consensus that recent body-mind studies have opened the door to many possibilities that would have been inconceivable within the framework of biomedicine. The reform movements of holistic and behavioral medicine have generated interest in the mind techniques of hypnosis, imagery, biofeedback, relaxation, and various forms of meditation. Though exaggerated claims about the powers of the mind abound, there is solid evidence that meeting spiritual needs (e.g., love and relatedness) is an important aspect of health care. The best-known and most-respected proponent of this position is the late Norman Cousins, whose recent book, *Head First*, tells the story of his ten-year stay at the UCLA School of Medicine as an advocate of the health-enhancing effects of hope and faith.[4]

The definition of faith that informs this search for a "faith factor" in medicine is broad and generic. It is faith understood as "ultimate concern" (Paul Tillich) or as trust in and loyalty to "centers of value and power" (James Fowler). Faith so defined is a human universal. It will be helpful to keep in mind a distinction between the "how" of faith and the "what" of faith. The "how" of faith refers to how one believes, for example, the experience of trust. The what of faith refers to what a person trusts or believes, for example, the acts of God, medical treatment, witchcraft. When Benson says that faith is a factor in healing, he is referring to "how" faith works within a person's psycho-physical organ-

4. Norman Cousins, *Head First: The Biology of Hope and the Healing Power of the Human Spirit* (New York: Penguin Books, 1990).

3

ism. "What" the person believes is of critical importance in analyzing the faith factor from a religious point of view.

After an overview of the expanding boundaries of modern medicine in Chapter 1, we will examine the first of three different areas of medicine in which a faith factor is prominent. The placebo effect refers to the patient's attitude and belief about the treatment he or she is receiving, be it medicine, anointing with oil, or some form of psychic healing. The faith factor is expectant trust, and it facilitates healing in ways that are sometimes quite remarkable.

A subtler example of the role of faith in medicine can be found in stories of illness, stories that go beyond the case histories that are a standard part of medical treatment. Thoughtful medical authors are advocating that physicians listen to the full story of illness before making interpretations (diagnoses) and prescribing treatment. It is in this expanded form of case history that faith as meaning-making emerges as a factor in the healing of persons (not just bodies).

Imagery has gained wide acceptance as a technique in medical care. Benson's relaxation response is a case in point. The faith factor can be discerned in the content of the imagery and the context in which it is used. Imagery utilizes images and symbols of faith to facilitate healing as a parallel method to the technical or material intervention of traditional medicine. After a descriptive analysis of a faith factor in imagery as practiced in medical and other non-Christian settings, I will argue for the use of religious imagery in a ministry of healing.

Completion of this project was made possible by a sabbatical leave from Valparaiso University and appointment as University Research Professor from 1988 to 1989, supplemented by the O.P. Kretzmann Memorial Scholarship, which is awarded annually to a member of the Valparaiso University faculty for study in the healing arts and is funded by the Wheatridge Foundation. I am also grateful to Dr. Lewis Spitz of Stanford University for assisting me in obtaining visiting scholar status at this superb educational institution.

4

A very special word of thanks to a wonderfully diverse group of people who read the manuscript: two physicians, Constance Covington and William Foege; a spiritual director, Robert Perry; a general semanticist, William Dallman; an English scholar, Elizabeth Droege; a professor of pastoral care, Elaine J. Ramshaw; and a philosopher, Paula Droege. Their feedback from a variety of perspectives was immensely helpful, but of course I accept full responsibility for the final product.

Finally, I dedicate this book to Wolfgang F. Bulle, M.D., who, along with Edward May (then director of the Wheatridge Foundation), first enlisted me in the cause of the church's healing ministry by asking me to serve as the study director of a medical mission conference in Coonoor, South India, in 1967. A dedicated medical missionary and director of many overseas medical programs, Dr. Bulle has been for me and many others a model of what the church's healing ministry is all about.

1

THE EXPANDING BOUNDARIES OF MODERN MEDICINE

The boundary between care of the soul and care of the body has been clearly defined for centuries in the Western world. Acceptance of the boundary by both religion and medicine has kept conflict at a minimum except when one invaded the territory of the other (e.g., the refusal of blood transfusions by Jehovah's Witnesses). Such disputes have been relatively rare. For the most part medicine has been content to remain within its domain of physical diagnosis/treatment and religion within its domain of spiritual care.

The philosophy of modern medicine can be traced to René Descartes, who argued that the material world operates according to mechanical laws and without reference to meaning and purpose: "I consider the human body as a machine. . . . My thought . . . compares a sick man and ill-made clock with my idea of a healthy man and a well-made clock." Since this mechanistic causality applies only to the body and not to the mind, health and spirituality have no common ground or potential for interaction.

The logic of Descartes' philosophy leads inevitably to the biomedical model that has become the dominant, almost exclusive paradigm for understanding health and healing in the Western world. A paradigm determines not only how we interpret what we see but even what we see. In addition, it is embedded so deeply within our psyche that few of us are aware of how determinative it is for the way we think about health and healing.

The scientific strategy of biomedicine is to reduce medicine to physiology, and the function of the body to molecular mechanisms. Disease, including mental illness, is disruption at the level of physiology. The scientific method is ideally suited to determine specific disease causation, and objectivity is a prerequisite for its use. When doing a case history, the physician is interested not in the "story" of the illness but in the facts that make for an accurate diagnosis. Not only does this emphasis on objectivity mask the importance of the physician-patient relationship as a factor in healing, but it also encourages patients to think of their bodies as objects. The impersonal, ahistorical, and acultural character of medicine are all related to its emphasis on objectivity.

There are signs of significant change. The boundary between medicine and religion is shifting. It is no longer obvious that the body can be studied objectively as a mechanism that functions independently from the mind or that faith is a factor that affects only the destiny of the soul. Studies in mind-body interaction too numerous to ignore are forcing medical scientists to reconsider the adequacy of the biomedical model that has for so long dictated both theory and practice. At the same time, studies lifting up the "faith factor" in healing make it clear that religion has reason to reclaim its ancient heritage of healing both body and soul.

Body and Mind— ### Discerning the Relationships

Evidence for body-mind communication comes from many quarters, some of it quite ancient, such as the scientifically documented ability of yogis in the Himalayas to control temperature and blood flow. Our modern version of this is biofeedback, now standard medical therapy. Almost all ancient methods of healing are evidence of body-mind communication, but examples that are familiar to us are likely to be more convincing.

It is common knowledge that warts can be removed through a variety of bizarre techniques. How is that possible? Lewis Thomas, well-known medical commentator, observes that warts "can be made to go away by something called thinking, or something like thinking. This is a special property of warts which is absolutely astonishing, more of a surprise than cloning or recombinant DNA or endorphins or acupuncture or anything else currently attracting attention in the press." Among its accomplishments this "healer from within" must be a surgeon, a skilled engineer and manager, a chief executive officer, and a cell biologist of world class. If we know how a wart was thought away, "we would be finding out about a kind of superintelligence that exists in each of us, infinitely smarter and possessed of technical know-how far beyond our present understanding."[1]

Even more remarkable is a well-documented case about the treatment by hypnosis of a sixteen-year-old youth with "fish-skin" disease. Treatment began with the left arm. Within five days the hard, horny layer of skin began softening and falling off. Within ten days the entire arm was normal in color and texture where before it had been thick, black, and covered with small, nipple-like projections as on the tongue. Other parts of the boy's body responded to treatment in an equally dramatic way. Four years later the original improvement was still present, and there was even some additional improvement. Similar results have been reported in other cases of the same disease.

Such results are rare. What can account for the exceptional ability of some people to influence their bodies through their minds? What is their unique gift? Theodore Barber, who examined the literature on hypnosis with this question in mind, contends that it is the ability to imagine with great vividness that characterizes those persons who have such exceptional ability. For such people an imagined event can be as vivid and seemingly as real as an actual event. They can imagine hearing music, seeing persons or objects, and experiencing themselves in the future or in the distant past. Thus, a vivid imagination appears to be a key factor in all so-called mind cures, whether by hypnosis, biofeedback, faith healing, the placebo effect, or guided imagery.

Instrumentation for measuring body-mind communication is at an early state of development, the findings striking but incon-

1. Lewis Thomas, *The Medusa and the Snail* (New York: Bantam Books, 1980), pp. 63–65.

clusive. What we do know at this early stage of research is that the body is much more responsive to emotions than to reason. Emotions are linked to the limbic system common to all mammals. The limbic system contains the hypothalamus, the "brain of the brain," which regulates appetite, drinking, sleeping, waking, body temperature, hormone balances, heart rate, sex drive, and emotions. The hypothalamus also directs the master gland of the brain, the pituitary. The pituitary gland regulates the body through hormones that are carried through the blood to cells especially equipped to receive the instructions communicated by them.

Messages are sent by brain cells in the form of neurotransmitters, which are "heard" by receiving cells that have receptors on their surface membranes. This provides the biological grounding for the theory that stress generated by a negative view of problems can be communicated to the body through scores of neuropeptides and their receptors.

Psychoneuroimmunology—
Medicine's New Frontier

The branch of medicine that has been the most deeply affected by studies on body-mind communication is immunology. Psychoneuroimmunology (PNI), a new branch of behavioral medicine, examines the relationship between the central nervous system, which can be affected by behavioral factors such as stress, and the immune system. The research in this area has been so thoroughly documented that PNI is an accepted subdiscipline within immunology.

Robert Ader, who gave this field its name and has been one of its top research scientists, stumbled onto the connection between behavior and immune function quite by accident. He was trying to instill in rats a conditioned aversion to saccharin-flavored water by pairing it with the drug cyclophosphamide, which made them feel nauseous. The rats were first given the flavored water to drink and then were injected with the drug. Very quickly they associated the taste of the sweetened water with the nausea. What troubled Ader was that the animals were dying for no obvious reason long after the drug had been out of their systems. Ader studied the effects of the drug and found that in addition to inducing nausea it also suppressed the immune system. For the conditioned animals, a taste of sweet water had the same effect as a dose of cyclophosphamide.[2] Repeated experiments by Ader and others skeptical of his findings produced the same result.

Those doing research in PNI operate with the assumption that the biological organism of humans is an open system in dynamic interaction with the environment. PNI calls for a multidisciplinary approach in an attempt to discern all the factors (physical, psychological, social) that may exert some influence on the immune response. Several thousand scientific articles published over the last decade broadly relate to this topic. Though many of the findings are unclear, and some even contradictory, nobody disputes the fact that the immune, endocrine, and central nervous systems of the body are interconnected.

The clearest and most striking evidence of such connections comes from studies of people with multiple personalities. The studies indicate that physical changes occur as personalities shift. In one case doctors had problems diagnosing and treating a woman admitted to the hospital with diabetic symptoms because the symptoms appeared only when a specific personality was in charge. In another case a man had allergic reactions to citrus fruit only when certain personalities dominated. The variable here is obviously not the body and its mechanisms (e.g., immune function), but the self as constituted by psychosocial factors.

The psychosocial influences can be both negative and positive. The negative influence is stress. One example is bereavement. It has been known for some time that persons who are grieving the death of a spouse, especially after many long years of marriage, are much more vulnerable to illness and death than those of simi-

2. Robert Ader and Nicholas Cohen, "Behaviorally Conditioned Immunosuppression and Murine Systemic Lupus Erythematosus," *Science* 215 (1982): 1534–36.

lar age and social status. Some have attributed this increased risk to poor eating and sleeping habits. An additional factor is a depressed immune system known to accompany the high stress of intense periods of bereavement.

In a classic animal study on the effects of stress, cancer researcher Vernon Riley demonstrated that even relatively benign stress can weaken an animal's disease resistance. He used a strain of mice genetically programmed to develop breast tumors. Riley made sure that his rats were placed in an environment that was as stress-free as he could make it (individual living quarters, temperature controlled, quiet). He then subjected the mice to a series of stress experiments to determine how the stress would affect the growth of the cancer they were bred to contract. The stress came from placing the mice in a cage attached to the top of a multispeed record turntable and spinning them around. He divided the mice into four groups, rotating at speeds from 16 revolutions per minute to 78 revolutions per minute. The faster the rotation, the greater the growth in the tumors, even though the animals seemed to adapt quite well— eating, drinking, and even mating at the various speeds.[3]

In another study rats were implanted with a tumor preparation and the next day received inescapable or escapable electric shocks or no electric shocks at all. The percentages of rats rejecting the tumors were 54 percent of those receiving no shock, 63 percent of those receiving escapable shock, and 27 percent of those receiving inescapable shock. These findings are supported by changes in immune function.[4]

If stress is a negative influence on the immune system, then what can serve as a positive influence? Evidence from current research suggests that positive imagery, for example, images of faith, can be such an influence. The best known but most controversial evidence of the positive effects of imagery on the immune system comes from the research done by O. Carl Simonton and

3. Vernon Riley, "Psychoneuroendocrine Influences on Immunocompetence and Neoplasia," *Science* 212 (1981): 1100–1109.
4. V. Riley, M. Fitzmaurice, and D. Spackman, "Psychoneuroimmunologic Factors in Neoplasia: Studies in Animals," in *Psychoneuroimmunology*, ed. Robert Ader (New York: Academic Press, 1981).

Stephanie Matthews-Simonton on their use of imagery in cancer therapy. Their book, *Getting Well Again*[5], generated enormous interest around the country in the use of imagery for healing. Current research in PNI demands more rigorous scientific standards than those used in the Simonton studies, but the body-mind communication suggested in those studies has received solid support.

Health and Spirituality

I have chosen recent studies in body-mind communication as an example of the expanding boundaries of modern medicine. Other examples could serve as well, such as the reform movement of holistic health care. There are some who argue for a radically new model for medicine in the upcoming century. That is not my concern. My interest is in the spirituality of health and healing, a domain that lies somewhere between the borders of medicine and religion.

The boundary lines between medicine and religion can be regarded either as the place where the two touch and influence each other or as a line of demarcation between two jealously guarded territories. In the one case the lines join and unite, in the other they divide and distinguish. In the past, making sharp distinctions has enabled medicine and religion to live in peaceful coexistence by respecting each other's turf. New discoveries in body-mind communication open up possibilities for exploring where the boundary lines join and unite. The key terms for this exploration are spirituality and faith.

Spirituality refers broadly to functions of the human spirit that distinguish a person from an animal: the capacity for reflection, for interpersonal relationships, for emotional attachments, for memory and anticipation, and for self-awareness. Only human beings have spiritual needs for love and relatedness, for forgiveness, for meaning, and for self-esteem.

5. O. Carl Simonton, Stephanie Matthews-Simonton, and James L. Creighton, *Getting Well Again* (New York: Bantam Books, 1978).

Those whose spiritual needs are not met will suffer spiritual maladies that are as serious and potentially destructive as physical maladies: depression, loneliness, existential anxiety, and meaninglessness. Spiritual care for such conditions calls for empathic listening, touching, loving, and forgiving. Not all of us are equally skilled in the art of spiritual care, though everyone practices the art to some degree within communal living. When spiritual maladies reach the point of making people dysfunctional, they call for professional care. In the past such care was exclusively religious in nature, but in our secularized society people often turn to psychotherapists, the secular priests of our modern age. The person to whom they go for help will depend both on how they perceive the nature of the malady and the kind of help they are seeking.

A distinction is needed between penultimate and ultimate ways in which spiritual needs are met. A spiritual need is being met when one person reaches out with love and support to a person who is lonely and depressed, but the care that is offered will be as limited and flawed as the person who provides it. Though that in no way negates the value of such care, it does point to the need for a sacral dimension to spiritual care that is neither limited nor flawed. The greatest deficit in spirituality in our modern era is not the lack of spiritual care (though such a lack does exist) but the limitations of a secularized spirituality. People yearn for a spirituality that is rooted in something more than the limited structures of interpersonal and communal caregiving. Not all spiritual care is religious, but religion is needed for spiritual care to fully satisfy the "wholeness hunger" of humanity.

Medicine is moving beyond its narrow biomedical base into the realm of secularized spirituality. Responsible health care calls for this movement, and religion should be strong in its affirmation of this shift toward more whole-person health care. The boundary line which religion must guard is not the boundary line between body and mind (spirit), but the boundary line between secularized and religious spirituality. It is this distinction that we will attend to carefully as we explore faith factors in the placebo effect, stories of illness, and the use of imagery in healing.

Faith is the specific form that spirituality takes in a particular individual or group. To use my earlier language, the term "faith" denotes both the structure and the content of a person's spirituality, both the experience of the person (e.g., trust) and what the person trusts (e.g., a physician or Christ). As with spirituality, there are both ultimate and penultimate forms of faith. Religion must guard the boundary line between these rather than argue that spirituality is its sole domain.

2

THE PLACEBO EFFECT—
FAITH HEALING IN
MEDICINE

The average physician would cringe at being called a "faith healer." Yet the physicians are faith healers in the sense that they invite expectant trust on the part of those who come for treatment. The white coat, the stethoscope, the prescription pad, the elaborate equipment in clinic and hospital, and the supreme self-confidence on the part of the physician all contribute to the faith people have in their doctors and in the health care system the doctors administer. The greater the threat that sick people feel, the more they need powerful symbols of authority to reinforce a belief that medicine can work wonders in reversing the course of illness.

This applies to all forms of healing, of course, whether it be Christian Science, Pentecostal healing, shamanism, or prayer. Called the "placebo effect" in medicine, the faith that people have in the treatment they are receiving is an important factor in healing, wherever it occurs. On the boundary line between religion and medicine, the placebo effect receives a great deal of attention in the medical literature but is virtually ignored by religion. That seems strange since the placebo effect is a matter of faith, not science. After demonstrating the effect of placebos in medical treatment, I will show the relationship of the placebo effect to faith, as understood from a religious perspective. Finally, I will argue that Christians need to rediscover what is so clear in the ministry of Christ, that faith is active in healing.

The Placebo Effect in Medicine

Placebo literally means "I shall please," a meaning reflected in Webster's dictionary: "A medicine ... given merely to satisfy a patient." A more adequate definition comes from Howard Brody: "A *placebo* is defined as any therapy ... that is deliberately used for its nonspecific psychologic or psychophysiologic effect, or that is used for its presumed effect on a patient, symptom or illness, but which, unknown to patient and therapist, is without specific activity for the condition being treated."[1] When used as a control in experimental studies, *placebo* is defined as a substance or procedure that has no known therapeutic value for the condition being evaluated.

As noted frequently in the literature, the history of medical treatment before the Enlightenment is the history of the placebo effect. Most medications prescribed by physicians were either pharmacologically inert or downright harmful. That physicians were prescribing placebos without knowing it only escalated their effectiveness. Some, however, were well aware of what they were doing. Robert Burton, a highly respected seventeenth-century physician, defended the use of spells, charms, and the like. "All the world knows there is no vertue in such charms," argued Burton, except for their power to dominate the imagination, "which forceth a motion of the humors, spirits, and blood, which takes away the cause of the malady from the parts affected. The like we say of all our magicall effects ... [which] doth more strange cures than a rationall Physition."[2]

After the Cartesian revolution, physicians who suggested that mental influences affect the body were regarded as quacks. The numerous citations of imagination-related illnesses and cures cited by William Falconer and D. H. Tuke a century later were regarded as nothing more than medical curiosities by their contemporaries.

1. Howard Brody, *Placebos and the Philosophy of Medicine: Clinical, Conceptual, and Ethical Issues* (Chicago: University of Chicago Press, 1980), p. 10.
2. Robert Burton, *The Anatomy of Melancholy* (Oxford: John Lichfield and James Short, 1621), p. 124.

Controlled clinical trials have forced the modern medical community to recognize the importance of the placebo effect, and it has recently been given the scholarly attention it deserves. Brody quotes Shapiro on the extensiveness of the placebo effect and the importance it has for the practice of medicine:

> Many papers have demonstrated the importance and magnitude of the placebo effect in every therapeutic area. Placebos can be more powerful than, and reverse the action of, potent active drugs. The incidence of placebo reactions approaches 100 percent in some studies. Placebos can have profound effects on organic illnesses, including incurable malignancies. Placebos can often mimic the effects of active drugs. Uncontrolled studies of drug efficacy are reported effective four to five times more frequently than controlled studies. Placebo effects are so omnipresent that if they are not reported in controlled studies it is commonly accepted that the studies are unreliable. Increased appreciation of placebo effects is reflected in the speculation that the major medical achievement of the last decade will be recorded by future medical historians as the development of methodology and controlled experiments.[3]

There are at least three dimensions of belief that are operative in the placebo effect of medical treatment: (1) the patient's belief in the method, (2) the physician's belief in the method, and (3) the patient's and physician's belief in each other. If all those factors are working optimally, even bizarre treatment procedures can produce real cures. If the opposite is true, even the most scientific and rational treatments may fail to cure. The patient's beliefs obviously receive most of the attention in the study of placebos, but the importance of the physician's belief in the therapeutic process needs emphasis as well.

A famous medical maxim attributed to Sir William Osler reads: "One should use a new remedy as much as possible while it still has the power to heal." It is the enthusiasm of the physician that a new "wonder" drug will be a powerful weapon in the battle with disease that accounts for the strong placebo effect of a new remedy. This effect is illustrated by a physician who

3. Brody, *Placebos and the Philosophy of Medicine*, pp. 10f.

prescribed an experimental drug for a patient's severe asthma. The patient reported marked relief in symptoms and showed improvement on lung function tests. Wondering what was drug and what placebo, the doctor substituted a placebo for the experimental drug. The patient's condition returned to what it had previously been. So the doctor requested an additional supply of the experimental drug. He was informed by the drug company that the "effective" experimental drug was, in fact, a placebo. It seems clear that the patient responded to the doctor's differing expectations, probably communicated in subtle ways: tone of voice, choice of words, and facial expressions.

Because of its checkered past, there are a number of misconceptions surrounding the placebo and its effects. The most pervasive among them is that the placebo effect is "all in a person's head." The fact is that physiological processes that can be objectively measured are affected in both organic and functional diseases. A second misconception is that only neurotic and suggestible people respond to placebos. The truth is that the placebo effect is a factor in all healing where a person is responding under conditions that evoke expectant trust. A third misconception is that the placebo effect is a nuisance factor that needs to be eliminated from clinical practice. The fact is that placebos are, on the average, 35 percent effective. This may be a nuisance factor for a researcher who wants to determine the effectiveness of an active pharmacological agent in the treatment of a disease, but anything that facilitates healing ought to be studied and promoted. Finally, it is a misconception to limit the placebo effect to occasions when patients think they are receiving medical treatment but are not. The fact is that any intervention that enhances positive expectations elicits the placebo response.

I have already indicated that the placebo effect is a factor in all healing. But under what conditions is the placebo response likely to be most effective? Howard Brody has identified three distinguishable but closely related components that contribute to a powerful placebo response.[4] First, the illness experience must be

4. Howard Brody, *Stories of Sickness* (New Haven, Conn.: Yale University Press, 1987), pp. 6f.

given an explanation of the sort that will be viewed as acceptable, given the patient's existing belief system (e.g., medical science, Christian Science, shamanism). Second, the patient must perceive that he or she is surrounded by and may rely upon a group of caring individuals. Third, the patient must achieve a sense of mastery or control over the illness experience, either by feeling personally powerful enough or by relying on the power of others, such as the physician or God.

Under the right conditions a placebo can contribute to negative as well as positive outcomes. The extreme example is a "voodoo death" that results from a combination of belief in magic, social withdrawal by family and friends, and a feeling of total inability to control or alter events. Contrast this to the reassurance provided by a physician that one's symptoms are caused by a bug going around, coupled with the caring attitude of physician and others who place one lovingly into a sick role, along with reassuring rituals (take two aspirin, etc.) that affirm control. Mothers as well as physicians heal in this way, as do clergy and others perceived as healers vested with authority and power.

Examples of the Placebo Effect

There are many examples of the placebo effect in the medical literature, both individual stories and research studies. The single most often quoted story comes from Bruno Klopfer, a physician and research scientist who tells about a radical cancer cure that can only be accounted for by the placebo effect. The story is about a man who had cancer of the lymph nodes. Standard treatments had been tried and failed. His body was filled with tumors, some the size of oranges. Every day one to two quarts of milky fluid were drained from his chest. He was in the terminal stage of cancer, and the treatment regimen was to make him as comfortable as possible.

But the patient was not ready to die. He heard that Krebiozen, touted as a new wonder cure, was being tested at the hospital where he had been sent to die. Though turned down by the study committee as being too close to death to be a good subject for the study, the patient cajoled them into giving him the drug. His physician reported on the results:

> The tumor masses had melted like snowballs on a hot stove, and in only these few days, they were half their original size! This is, of course, far more rapid regression than most radiosensitive tumors could display under heavy X-ray given most every day. And we already knew his tumor was no longer sensitive to irradiation. Also he had no other treatment outside of the since useless "shot." Mr. Wright left the hospital practically symptom free, and even flew his own plane at 12,000 feet with no discomfort.[5]

The shot was "useless" because reports began to appear in the press to the effect that Krebiozen was ineffectual. His faith weakened, Mr. Wright had a relapse after enjoying two months of relatively good health and was readmitted to the hospital. Since there was obviously more than biochemistry involved in this case, his physicians decided to enhance the placebo effect that they felt sure was operative in his dramatic recovery. Mr. Wright was told that he would receive a double-strength dosage of a new, improved type of Krebiozen. What he really received was an injection of pure water. Klopfer reports that "recovery from his second near-terminal state was even more dramatic than the first. Tumor masses melted, chest fluid vanished, he became ambulatory, and even went back to flying again."[6] This second relapse ended when a newspaper account carried an announcement from the American Medical Association that "nationwide tests show Krebiozen to be a worthless drug in treatment of cancer." Mr. Wright died within days of the announcement.

This story attracts so much attention not only because of its high drama but also because it so clearly illustrates that the placebo effect is not limited to functional diseases, so named because they affect a function of some organ without apparent structural or organic changes. I must hasten to add, however, that this is a rare story, and we should be very cautious about drawing implications from this or any other isolated account of a dramatic cure.

5. Bruno Klopfer, "Psychological Variables in Human Cancer," *Journal of Prospective Techniques* 31 (1957): 334.
6. Ibid., p. 339.

One more individual report on the power of the placebo is worth citing because the person's expectations were shown to affect physiological responses powerfully enough to reverse the pharmacological action of a drug. The drug ipecac normally causes cessation of stomach contractions shortly after ingestion. The patient experiences this as nausea. "A pregnant patient suffering from excessive vomiting showed the normal response of cessation of stomach contractions with nausea and vomiting after receiving a dose of ipecac. When the same medication was given to her through a tube, so that she did not know what it was, with strong assurance that it would cure her vomiting, gastric contractions started up at the same interval after its administration that they would normally have stopped, and simultaneously the patient's nausea ceased."[7]

Research studies are more persuasive than anecdotes because of the number of cases and the control of variables. One of the most interesting studies, conducted by two Japanese researchers, showed the inhibition or triggering of allergic skin reactions by suggestion alone. Thirteen high school boys known to be highly allergic to certain plants were asked to participate in the experiment, which was conducted by a well-respected physician in a respected medical setting. After being instructed to close their eyes, the boys were told by the physician that the leaves of the harmless plant he was brushing over their arms was the plant to which they were allergic. All thirteen of the boys demonstrated some degree of dermatitis (including itching, redness, papules, swelling, and blisters). Then the boys were told that they were being touched by the leaves of a harmless plant when in fact the leaves were poisonous. Eleven of the thirteen did not show the expected dermatitis.[8] Only the placebo effect can account for these results.

Among the medical treatments likely to be enhanced by the placebo effect, surgery is at the top of the list, probably because there is so much drama and ritual associated with it (hospitaliza-

---

7. Jerome Franks, *Persuasion and Healing* (New York: Schocken Books, 1961), p. 67.
8. Y. Ikemi and S. Nakagawa, "A Psychosomatic Study of Contagious Dermatitis," *Journal of Medical Science* 13 (1962): 335–52.

tion, operating "theater," masked and green-robed surgical team, induction by anesthesia). In the mid-1950s, for example, a new surgical procedure was introduced to provide relief from symptoms of chest pain due to coronary heart disease. The procedure was called "internal mammary ligation" and involved tying off an artery in the chest. One out of three patients reported complete relief of pain while three out of four reported some improvement. Since this procedure was considered successful, ten thousand operations followed.

Some surgeons were skeptical about the procedure because there seemed to be no sound physiological basis for the treatment, especially since the relief from pain was almost immediate, long before new vessels could have provided a fresh supply of blood to the heart. In a study that would be considered unethical by today's standards, seventeen patients severely limited by angina were recruited to do an evaluation of the procedure. They did not know they were participating in a double-blind study in which they were randomly assigned to receive either that operation or a sham operation. In both cases an incision was made in the chest. Patients in one group had their arteries tied while the others were simply closed up with no surgery performed—a placebo operation. The benefits from the placebo surgery were as great as the artery-tying operation. After these results were confirmed by a replicated study, the operation was abandoned.

Examples of the negative effects of placebos are also plentiful. The most dramatic examples are stories of voodoo death— people in primitive cultures who die within days after being hexed by a witch doctor. It may be difficult for us to identify with the victims of such a curse because the belief system that gives it power is so foreign to us. Bernard Lown, professor of cardiology at Harvard, tells a story about a similar kind of phenomenon that could have happened to anybody. Early in his career, Lown witnessed his chief examining on clinical rounds a middle-aged woman who had congestive heart failure and swelling in the ankles from an accumulation of fluid. Her condition did not keep her from work or attending to household chores. Lown's mentor turned to the entourage of physicians following him and announced, "This woman has TS." He had hardly gone out the door before the woman began breathing rapidly, became drenched with perspiration, and had a pulse rate of more than 150 beats a minute. Lown quickly examined her and found that her lungs, which had been clear, now had an accumulation of fluid. He asked her why she was so upset. With a knowing look, the woman said that she was aware that TS meant "terminal situation." Lown tried to reassure her that it meant "tricuspid stenosis," a narrowing of the tricuspid heart valve, and that she was not in a terminal condition. Despite his efforts, the woman died the same day from heart failure.[9]

Why Placebos Work

All of the above examples demonstrate the pervasiveness and the power of the placebo for both facilitating and obstructing healing. But how does it work? The traditional medical explanation is that placebos affect functional or psychosomatic disorders but not disease, which refers to a pathological condition that has structural manifestations in the organism (e.g., a broken leg or a brain tumor). Subjective complaints are relieved, but diseases are not changed. Most of the gains credited to the placebo effect are the result of self-limiting diseases or spontaneous remissions. Orthodox medical opinion is particularly critical of isolated reports of the placebo effect, though the data from clinical trials offer unquestioned scientific proof of its healing power.

Given the limits of the conceptual framework within which biomedical analysis takes place, it is no wonder that the placebo effect is judged as having nothing to do with the "real" business of medicine, which is to intervene in a disease process that operates in a quite mindless way. We need to look elsewhere for more convincing alternative explanations.

The most common explanation of the placebo effect is suggestion, the patient's expectation of change being causally connected to the subsequent change. Some form of body-mind communica-

9. Bernard Lown, Introduction, in Norman Cousins, *The Healing Heart* (New York: Norton Books, 1983), pp. 11–28.

tion, operating in the deep structures of the brain, underlies this change. We cannot just will ourselves to be healthy. Nor are we likely to be conscious of the ways we block healing, stress our bodies, or send negative mental images to our bodies. As noted in Chapter 1, we know much more about this kind of communication and how it affects healing than ever before, though we are probably seeing only the tip of the iceberg at this point.

However, we do have clear scientific evidence for how suggestion works, at least in the relief of pain, from an experiment done by researchers at the University of California in San Francisco. They studied postoperative pain in fifty-one men and women undergoing surgical removal of impacted wisdom teeth. After the teeth were removed under standard anesthesia, the patients spent several hours in a recovery room where they all received a randomly selected injection of morphine, naloxone, or a placebo. Opiate receptors in the brain are the key to the control of pain. Morphine works because it has the chemical key to lock in to these receptors. The drug naloxone can block this action because it can literally knock out the morphine and lock in to the receptors without activating the cell. The body's own morphine is called endorphin (endogenous morphine). In times of stress the body releases endorphins to kill pain and allow the body to meet whatever emergency is there.

The dental patients who received placebos in the University of California experiment were classified as responders and non-responders, the responders being those who had a positive response to the administration of a placebo. The responders noted a significant increase in the level of pain when they received a heavy dose of naloxone subsequent to the placebo injection, while the nonresponders noted no change. This demonstrates that a major part of placebo analgesia is mediated by the production of endorphins since naloxone blocks the effects of opiates and endorphins.

Conditioning is another possible explanation for how placebos work. Have you ever had the experience of no longer feeling ill while you were waiting to see your doctor and wondering why you made an appointment in the first place? You associate this medical setting with the relief of symptoms that came with previous treatments received there. Later, the setting itself is sufficient stimulus to initiate the healing response.

Both of the above explanations, though persuasive, are limited in scope. Howard Brody, both a physician and a philosopher, offers a much more comprehensive and penetrating interpretation of how the placebo effect works by placing it within the framework of the meaning of life. According to Brody, all healing practices have two invariant features related to meaning: (1) a belief system that explains illness in terms (natural or supernatural) readily understandable to those who share the same way of looking at the world, and (2) a relationship with a socially sanctioned healer occupying a role with parental-like power and influence, which in turn stimulates caring responses from family and community. These two factors, both essential for the experience of meaning, are "the necessary and sufficient components of the placebo effect."[10]

Most of the research on the type of person who responds to placebos has focused on personality variables, such as being noncritical or highly suggestible. Little attention has been given to the belief systems of placebo responders. It is the combination of belief system and sanctioned healer that gives one a sense of mastery and control over the illness. The person's belief system may be true or false and the sense of control well-founded or illusory. The point is that the belief system that gives meaning to a person's life is an important factor in the healing process.

Brody proposes a view of human nature that is similar to religious views when he defines persons as animals possessing the ability to use symbols in such a way that the use confers meaning upon the symbol. Persons so defined are both biological and cultural beings. Brody applies this philosophical/theological construction to the placebo effect:

> Our subject who experiences the placebo effect is no longer a mind and a body, but is a person. Being a person entails having all the capacities of a biological organism, and in addition the special

10. Brody, *Placebos and the Philosophy of Medicine*, p. 24.

THE FAITH FACTOR IN HEALING

capacity to be a symbol user and necessarily a dweller within culture. If being a dweller within culture is a special way of being an animal, it should not be anomalous if this characteristic were found to influence other animal capacities—including the capacities to undergo changes in bodily status and function. Symptom change caused by the placebo effect is therefore the bodily expression of the person's participation in the healing context understood as a culturally determined, symbolic phenomenon.[11]

So long as medicine limits its perspective to physiology, where the only allowable analogy is to the physiology of other animals, biomedicine can only view the placebo effect as an anomaly that needs to be explained away. But if persons are *essentially* both biological and cultural beings, the cultural aspect will influence the biological aspect and vice versa. Given this frame of reference, the placebo response is not only understandable but to be expected. Indeed, the lack of a placebo response might well be an indication of a need for healing in the realm of the spiritual.

Faith Active in Healing

Brody's philosophical analysis of the placebo effect provides a bridge to the religious analysis which follows. In the language that I am using in this study, I would describe the placebo response as a universal factor in healing. A clinical trial does not compare a material remedy with nothing; the comparison is with faith. We do not have similar studies that document the placebo response in Christian Science, Pentecostal healing, folk remedies, shamanism, or the use of magic, but it seems likely that the same faith element is an active healing agent in all of these practices.

I am not suggesting that all or even most of the healing in these practices can be explained by the placebo response, only that it is a factor in all healing. The faith factor refers not to the content of faith but to its structure—the nature and quality of believing. Viewed from this perspective, faith in God is no more effective as a placebo response than is faith in the doctor; the

11. Ibid., p. 81.

26

difference in effectiveness is the degree of expectant trust characteristic of each. This is why faith as a placebo response is likely to be more of a factor in medical treatment than in religious practices. Ask yourself whether you expect more healing from medical treatment than you do from prayer. Your answer will indicate where the placebo effect is likely to be stronger.

We cannot live without faith, as Luther reminded us. To be human is to need meaning and purpose in life. Philosophers and theologians have long noted the importance of a worldview or symbol system for bringing order, meaning, and purpose into the lives of persons and communities. What seems clear from our analysis thus far is that the faith which these belief systems evoke can facilitate healing and maintain wholeness. But does it make any difference what you believe? That is a crucial question that can only be answered from a religious perspective, and the remaining portion of the chapter will be devoted to it.

Among other things, what we believe makes a difference in how healing and wholeness are defined. Wholeness means physical wholeness in the symbol systems of both medicine and religion, but wholeness means much more than that from most religious perspectives. It is obvious that physical wholeness is threatened by illness and ended by death. That is why faith in medicine is of little value when death is imminent. From a medical perspective it would make no sense to speak of healing in relation to the dying of Jesus, though Christians affirm that his wounds are a source of healing. Furthermore, if achieving and maintaining physical health has become so important to a person that he or she organizes his or her whole life around it, then that person's faith is a form of idolatry when examined from a Christian perspective. That person is suffering from a malady much deeper than physical illness, and its end result is spiritual rather than physical death.

As is obvious from the last two paragraphs, what we believe is as important as the way we believe (e.g., the level of trust) for understanding the faith factor in healing. We will look more closely at the implications for the content of faith for healing in the next chapter when we examine the stories that give meaning to illness and health. For now I return to our analysis of the placebo effect and how that might best be utilized by persons whose vocation is spiritual healing rather than physical healing. More specifically, I will comment on how faith is understood and utilized by Christians in their rich tradition of healing.

For the most part, Christians do not look to their churches for healing. There are exceptions: Christian Science, the Pentecostal tradition (including the Charismatic movement), and many individual Christians who strongly believe in the power of God to heal in the here and now. These are, however, not representative of the mainstream of Christianity. What has eroded the faith of most Christians in God's power to heal through the church's ministry?

Cultural influences are largely responsible. We live in an age dominated by the prestige of science. Skepticism about any claim to healing that does not have a rational explanation reinforces faith in medicine and erodes faith in prayer and other forms of spiritual healing. Recent court cases against the use of Christian Science healing with children indicate the strength of this cultural bias which reinforces faith in medical care and undermines faith in forms of spiritual healing.

However, the primary reason for the erosion of faith in the power of God to heal is the virtual abandonment of a ministry of healing by the mainline churches. Acceptance of a sharp division between body and soul has been as characteristic of church doctrine as of medical theory. The counterpart to body reductionism is soul reductionism. Salvation, which means wholeness, is then reduced to life after death and faith to a transaction that gets you there. Given this approach, the church's ministry of healing becomes the "cure of souls," at the heart of which is the forgiveness of sins. Anointing with oil, originally a rite for the healing of the sick (James 5), becomes instead the preparation of the soul for its departure from the body. It is not surprising that the church has lived so comfortably and so long with the neat division of labor between religion and medicine.

What happens to the church's rich tradition of healing when faith has been factored out of it? Sermons on the healing stories in the Gospels are spiritualized by making a condition such as physical blindness symbolic of spiritual blindness. Prayers for healing, while still common, often do little to evoke faith because of their conditional nature ("if it be thy will") and the type of petitions (strength to endure, guidance, and blessing of medical endeavors). It is strange that God's promise to heal, so clear in the Gospels, is qualified in so many ways today. There is no such qualification of God's promise to forgive sins. Both are promises of the gospel and invite faith in return, but faith cannot be a factor if trust in the promise has been undermined.

The point of these comments is not that the church should once again encourage people to trust in God's promise to heal through prayer and anointing in order to enhance the placebo effect. It has negative rather than positive associations for most people both in and outside the medical community, implying deception on the part of the caregiver and gullibility on the part of the recipients of care. Within Christianity there is an even stronger reason for being suspicious of the placebo effect as a positive factor in healing.

It would appear that the placebo effect is due to human rather than divine agency. At the heart of the gospel message is the comforting assurance that we are saved because of God's gracious promise and not because of human endeavor. Thus Christians have been encouraged to trust in the promises of God rather than in the quality of their faith. The faith healing of the placebo response appears to be a form of self-healing that is different from and perhaps even opposed to the gracious working of God in our lives.

Thus the purpose in calling attention to the absence of a placebo effect in the church's ministry is not to propose bolstering people's expectations of being healed in order to prompt a placebo response on their part. The church has even less moral sanc tion for such deceit than does medicine. The purpose is rather to strengthen faith in the genuine promise of the gospel, which includes the promise of healing. When that promise goes unheeded, faith does not die. It turns elsewhere—to medicine, to New Age mysticism, to self-healing methodologies. The real question is where faith should be directed and how we think that God is acting in the world today.

A new awareness of the faith factor in healing challenges Christians to rethink some fundamental questions about the church's ancient and yet contemporary mission of healing. Has the practice of faith healing been relegated to fringe groups within the church? Is the scientific worldview so dominant in our age that the very idea of physical healing through spiritual means is rejected out of hand? Are Christians as guilty as those in the medical profession of stressing the passivity of the person in need of healing? Can a "natural" healing occur through a ministry that is spiritual?

While all those questions are worth exploring, it is the last one that deserves special attention in considering what to expect from the church's ministry of healing through word and sacrament. The idea of instant, miraculous healing by supernatural power makes many people, including myself, uneasy about faith healing. This is not a question about God's power to heal instantly. Nobody who believes in the resurrection could have any question about God's power to restore people to health by any means. But does it have to be miraculous to qualify as spiritual healing? I would argue that faith discovers the power of God at work wherever healing occurs and by whatever means. The expectant trust that Christians have in modern medical treatment can be an expression of their faith in the power of God at work in the realm of nature. Is the healing done in the name of Christ the same (natural) or different (supernatural) from that?

Christians witness to the unique historical embodiment of God's power to heal in the person of Jesus Christ. The Gospels are the primary witness to Christ the healer, but the promise of healing which Jesus embodies continues to be re-presented when the church heals in his name. The promise is not that God will heal instantly and supernaturally. The promise is that the divine compassion and healing presence that was embodied in Christ the healer is now mediated through the healing ministry of the church. The church gathers to pray, to hear the ancient stories of healing, to receive Christ through the ordinary means of water, bread, and wine, to anoint with oil and lay hands of healing on the sick. There is every reason to expect healing through this ministry, and in a manner that is as ordinary and natural as the healing that comes through medical intervention.

Do we minimize the power of God when we draw attention to ways in which healing takes place within the laws of nature, for example, images of faith communicating directly to the body via mind-body connections? The answer to that question is yes if it takes a miracle to get people's attention and prompt them to look beyond the event to its source in God. However, if it is the supernatural character of Jesus' healing stories that validates them as authentic and divine, then either healing was a gift for that age only or similar kinds of miracles are needed to validate the healing that is done in Christ's name today. I think that the fundamental distinction that we need to make is not between natural and supernatural, but between physical and spiritual methods of healing. Though those methods are very different from each other, the healing in both cases can be construed as a natural process.

I am addressing myself primarily to those who are skeptical about miracle cures today and do not want to link spiritual healing to such claims. The issue is not whether miracles occur or not, but whether spiritual healing should be based on claims that they do. I regard the matter of miracles to be an open question. Some expect instantaneous cures, others do not. There are valid arguments on both sides. These options need not be mutually exclusive. My contention is that some methods of spiritual healing (e.g., through imagery) can be both fully Christian and natural at the same time.

Images link mind and body. Imagery channels communication from the mind to the body via the limbic-hypothalamic system. Images (neural impulses) generated through right-brain access are filtered through the limbic-hypothalamic system and transduced into the neurotransmitters that regulate the autonomic, endocrine, and immune systems of the body. It is because imagery can communicate across the mind-body barrier that it is such a valuable resource for healing.

31

The content of imagery used for healing is varied, some of it secular, some of it based on a faith tradition other than Christianity, and some Christ-centered. The purpose of Christ-centered imagery is to deepen the experience of the presence and power of the healing Christ in the lives of people today. It is one thing to *talk about* the healing stories of Jesus that happened many years ago; it is quite another thing to *experience* the presence and power of the healing Christ in those stories by using one's imagination to go back to the first century or by reframing those stories as contemporary experiences. The first is a left-brain exercise. The second is a right-brain exercise. Since the right brain spawns images which can communicate directly with the body, there is power to heal through an imagery exercise that facilitates a deeper-than-intellectual faith experience.

As the experience of Christ the Healer deepens, so will the expectant trust of those who look to Christ for healing. Does the expectant trust, the faith factor in healing, contribute something in addition to God's power to heal? That is not the right question. It assumes the validity of a distinction between what God is doing (through Christ) and what humans are doing (through expectant trust). The truth is that we cannot take our analysis any further than to say that healing takes place within a relationship to God that is based on faith. Spiritual healing is relational, and the faith pole in this relationship is expectant trust.

Healing flows out of a relationship to Christ. Jesus told some people that their faith made them well, and in other instances Jesus could do no healing because of the lack of faith. Faith *is* a factor in healing, and for Christians it is attached to Christ the Healer. That's why the promises of God need to be vivid and compelling, inviting faith as the appropriate response.

The heavy emphasis that I have placed on faith as a factor in healing in no way implies that faith is the only factor in healing, be that physical or spiritual healing. That may seem more obvious in physical than spiritual healing since medical treatment is primarily a matter of material remedies. Though faith has always been acknowledged as a factor in spiritual healing, the power of God to heal through word and sacrament is at the center of spiritual healing. Faith is the point of connection to the power and presence of God, but by no means the controlling factor in the healing that flows from the power and presence of God.

Returning to the language that we have been using in this chapter, "faith" refers to the placebo effect, whether it be in medicine or in God. Though a medical term, "placebo" refers to the religious dimension of healing. Ironically, what we learn from medicine is the healing power of faith. It is a nuisance to medicine because it does not fit into the biomedical model. The placebo is at the core of religion because it reveals the object of one's faith. If one's faith is grounded only in medicine and what it can do, it is idolatrous.

The task of the church is to redirect the faith of its members to God, the source of all healing, medical or churchly. As Donald Shriver reminds us, "The medical profession would be ill served by members who do not appreciate the real powers of medicine. So also with the field of religion. 'Be not eager for self-negation,' medical people may need to say to students and practitioners of religion."[12] The placebo belongs to the "powers of religion." At issue is not how to elicit the placebo response but how to be properly cognizant of and responsive to the power of God to heal.

---

12. Donald W. Shriver, Jr., "The Interrelationships of Religion and Medicine," in *On Moral Medicine: Theological Perspectives in Medical Ethics*, ed. Stephen Lammers and Allen Verhey (Grand Rapids: Wm. B. Eerdmans, 1987), p. 14.

3

FRAMING OUR STORIES OF ILLNESS AND HEALING

In this chapter we will examine the still modest effort to expand the case history in medicine to a much broader "soul" history. Instead of mapping only the objective data of biological symptoms, the physician is encouraged to place the "disease" (organismic malfunction) within the larger context of the "illness" (the story of what it means and how the person is coping with it). Though case histories are as old as the medical profession, it is no small step for medicine to include the story of illness as data for diagnosis and treatment.

As soon as we attend to the stories by which people give meaning to illness and health, we are moving out of the traditional territory of medicine and into the humanities, and the stories about ultimate meaning are the "holy ground" of religion. That medicine should be attending to these broader concerns is cause for rejoicing. There is conflict with religion in this shift only if a health professional demeans a patient's story of illness and imposes his or her own version of what the story ought to be. It is one thing to support a patient's search for ultimate meaning and another to dictate the outcome of that search.

The Importance of a Comprehensive Framework of Meaning

We depend on all kinds of maps to know who we are and where we are going. We consult a state map if we want to make a trip to its capital, but there are also cognitive maps which represent for us what the world is really like. For example, every healing system has a map of the physical and metaphysical world that enables the people who use that map to name their diseases and seek appropriate healing remedies. Those who are wise know the fallacy of confusing the map with the territory. The information that we have about health, illness, and healing is limited, and so the map that we use to chart this territory is always in need of revision.

Medicine has a sophisticated map for diagnosing disease and prescribing treatment, and a physician is consulted because he or she is an expert in the interpretation of that map. The map is detailed and accurate, but it would be a grave error to assume that it is complete or that it is the only way that the territory can be mapped. For example, the medical map tells us much more about why people get sick than it does about why so many people stay well. We need a different map for that, or rather an overlay which enables us to discern the presence of illness as well as disease, healing as well as cure, wellness as well as health. In this chapter we will look at the difference it makes when we superimpose a larger map over the medical model to better understand what keeps people from getting sick and helps others survive longer and cope more effectively when they are ill.

What Keeps Us Well?

Louis Pasteur was a major contributor to the theory that germs cause disease, but he was also aware of what he called the "terrain" of disease, that is, the environmental factors that largely determine susceptibility and resistance to disease. Pasteur and Claude Bernard often debated whether the disease producer, the microbe, or the body's defenses were more important. On his deathbed Pasteur is reported to have said, "Bernard was right. The germ is nothing, the soil is everything." Medicine has operated as though the soil was nothing and the germ everything. In fact, medicine is closer to a disease care system than a health care system. Fortunately, this is beginning to change as studies show strong correlations between stress and the onset of disease and between effective coping and the maintenance of health.

Health care workers are not trained to assess what is right with a person. They examine a patient in the same way that one examines a drawing in the newspaper that has the caption, "What's wrong with this picture?" In fact, that is exactly what the diagnostician asks when looking at X-rays and other test results. It is not that we want to discourage the question about what is wrong. We are asking it ourselves when we go to the doctor. The problem is we ask questions about our body only when we are sick, and we expect answers only from physicians.

The standard procedure for correcting what is wrong with a person is to introduce an external agent, such as drugs or surgery, to effect some mechanical changes in the body. An alternative approach is to shift the focus of attention from the disease to the host and consider the personal strengths of the person and how they might be mobilized. That shift calls for a larger, more comprehensive map of the person than one used to chart the physiological function alone. It is to such a map that we now turn.

We begin with a definition of wellness as the capacity for restoring and maintaining order and balance within an organism that is always in a state of disequilibrium. Disorder is inevitable because of the multiple sources of stress, both internal and external in origin. Stress brings tension and disorder to every level of a person's functioning: biological, psychological, social, and spiritual.

That which enables us to maintain a dynamic state of balance is "a sense of coherence," which Aaron Antonovsky defines as a "feeling of confidence that one's internal and external environments are predictable and that there is a high probability that things will work out as well as can reasonably be expected."[1] We are constantly confronted with stimuli to which we have no automatic adaptive response. People with a strong sense of

1. Aaron Antonovsky, *Unraveling the Mysteries of Health: How People Manage Stress and Stay Well* (San Francisco: Jossey-Bass Publishers, 1987), p. xiii.

coherence are more likely to respond to stimuli realistically and are less likely to react to a source of stress as a threat to their well-being. They will seek to impose structure on a situation and have confidence in their self-sufficiency. People with a weak sense of coherence will see chaos, feel hopeless and burdened, and expect no good outcome. The difference is one of attitude, and once established, usually by early adulthood, it is likely to characterize one's stance toward the world throughout life.

Antonovsky identifies the following components of a sense of coherence from fifty-one in-depth interviews with a wide variety of persons:

1. Comprehensibility—the extent to which one perceives internal and external stimuli as information (ordered, consistent, structured, and clear) rather than as noise (chaotic, disordered, random, accidental, and inexplicable).
2. Manageability—the extent to which one perceives that resources are at one's disposal that are adequate to meet the demands posed by both external and internal stimuli. The resources may be under one's own control or controlled by others (e.g., God) whom one trusts to provide the needed control. A negative example is the "sad sack," to whom unfortunate things happen, always have and always will.
3. Meaningfulness—the extent to which life is important, something that people care about, that "makes sense" to them. Events, including changes with considerable stress, are seen as challenges worthy of emotional investment and commitment.[2]

In his research Antonovsky found that meaningfulness was the most important of the three components. Without it, comprehensibility and manageability were likely to be temporary. There are exceptions, however. In a time of crisis, for example, with the recurrence of cancer, the goal of healing will be manageability, helping the person regain control. Control implies acceptance of limitations plus an awareness that these very limitations open up the possibility for a deeper level of meaningfulness, that is, that

2. Ibid., pp. 15–22.

37

the ultimate control of both life and death lies in the hands of a gracious God.

Antonovsky argues persuasively for the importance of a strong sense of coherence, but as a social scientist he is not in a position to say how an illness can be made comprehensible, manageable, or meaningful. He does point the way, however, to a search for some ultimate way of grounding comprehensibility, manageability, and meaningfulness. That calls for a religious perspective, and later in the chapter I will show how Christians ground their sense of coherence in the gospel. First we turn to an analysis of the correlation between a sense of coherence and health.

<h3 style="text-align:center">Helplessness and Hopelessness:
Common Precursors to Illness</h3>

Before citing the compelling evidence for a strong positive correlation between a sense of coherence and health, we will look at studies which show that those who lack a sense of coherence are more likely to become ill and less likely to recover rapidly. Mounting research indicates that those who make internal, consistent, and global assumptions about the cause of bad things happening in their lives have an increased risk of illness. The assumption is "internal" in the sense that "I'm the cause of all my problems." The assumption becomes "consistent" in that "It will always be this way." The assumption becomes "global" when "It's going to spoil everything I do." A sense of helplessness and hopelessness regularly results when such overpersonalizing, overgeneralizing, and catastrophizing undermine a person's sense of coherence.

Animal studies provide evidence for this pattern of giving up when things seem totally out of control. When dogs are given unavoidable, inescapable electric shocks, they seem to accept their situation as hopeless, even when later placed into a shock situation that includes an opportunity to escape. The same is true of rats that are put into a situation from which they cannot flee or fight, such as being held under a bag or placed in a jar full of water. They quickly die from a slowing of the heart and respiration. That happens even more quickly if their whiskers, a principal source of sensing the environment and orienting them, have been clipped. However, if the rats are periodically and briefly put in a water jar and let go each time, they will later swim in the jar for long periods without signs of giving up or dying. The behavior of human beings is similar when the situation is perceived as uncontrollable and the outcome dire.

One striking example of the difference that a "hopeless" label makes is the story of a woman in a mental hospital who had remained mute for nearly ten years while residing in a unit that was known as the chronic, hopeless floor. While her unit was being redecorated, she was moved to a floor that was occupied by improved patients with privileges, including freedom to come and go on the hospital grounds. Soon the woman surprised everyone by ceasing to be mute and becoming socially responsive and gregarious. Within a week of being returned to the "hopeless" floor, she collapsed and died. The autopsy revealed no pathology of note.

Death by hopelessness can be inferred from the death rate of prisoners-of-war. Approximately 94,000 U.S. servicemen were taken prisoner in Europe during World War II. Most were imprisoned for an average of ten months and less than 1 percent died. Twenty-five thousand Americans were imprisoned in the Pacific, and they were tortured, threatened, abused, and humiliated. About one-third of these men died. Those who became listless, apathetic, and without hope were the persons most likely to die.

These accounts of what has been called "learned helplessness" are supported by dozens of studies which show that the people who were most likely to get sick had recently experienced some stressful situation that they perceived as being beyond their con trol, having no solution, or leaving them helpless. Studies predicting the effects of helplessness are only beginning to appear. One that is a model for future research was able to predict which of a large group of Army recruits might develop an ulcer during basic training. The recruits who were rated as having high dependency needs and experiencing high stress were most likely to develop an ulcer. Separated from home and people who took care of them, they were forced to give up gratifications which they could not bear to relinquish; they perceived themselves as helpless.

If helplessness and hopelessness contribute to illness and lessen the prospects of recovery, then hope that is grounded in a realistic assessment of the possible will be a vital ingredient for health and healing. Arnold Hutschnecker writes about the importance of hope as an active force in one's life:

> Active hope is an inner mental force that triggers the human will into action. It mobilizes an individual's vast energies in order to overcome obstacles that block his or her way toward a chosen goal. . . . Active hope balances our inner needs with the controlling demands of an often harsh reality. It also supplies us with the energies and reassurance necessary to safeguard the integrity of a healthy ego striving for wholesomeness.[3]

Active hope, which is an internal healing force rather than a passive waiting for something to happen, must always be grounded in what is possible and thus distinguished from wishful fantasy. For example, hope that is rooted in the promise of God to heal is an expression of faith, but expecting God to restore an arm or a leg that has been lost in an accident is wishful fantasy.

Sense of Coherence: An Indicator of Wellness

Hope contributes to a sense of coherence, and there is considerable evidence to support a correlation between a strong sense of coherence and high levels of wellness. A twenty-year study was done of 700 children growing up in Hawaii.[4] All came from poor families. They were followed from a few months before birth to their early twenties—during a period of great social change. These were children of high risk, but many of them survived and

3. Arnold A. Hutschnecker, *Hope: The Dynamics of Self-fulfillment* (New York: G. P. Putnam's Sons, 1981), p. 16.
4. Emmy E. Werner and Ruth S. Smith, *Vulnerable, but Invincible: A Study of Resilient Children* (New York: McGraw-Hill, 1982).

even thrived in the face of adversity and extreme stress. Common characteristics among these children were positive self-concept, sense of responsibility, achievement-orientation, and a sense of coherence. One of the key findings of this study is that stress does not always contribute to disease. Stress is like a germ, an external agent that contributes to disease only when the host cannot adapt. Stress-resistant people need change and challenge and will seek out novelty and stimulation.

Another study of people who remain well in spite of high stress was done on a group of middle- and upper-level business executives. There was a greater incidence of disease among those who scored high on a stress scale. The high stress/low illness group was characterized by a strong commitment to self, work, family, and other central values, a sense of control over their lives even when threatened by chaos, and the ability to see change in their lives as a challenge rather than a threat. These three traits made for psychological hardiness. Hardy executives also seemed to take better advantage of social support to protect their health. Executives low in hardiness, on the other hand, appeared to be disadvantaged by strong emotional support, perhaps because of a tendency to retreat into the supportive world and hide.

Evidence for the role that religious faith plays as a coping device comes from a study by a hospital chaplain of the relationship between the healing time of patients after retinal detachment surgery and their methods of coping. The study showed that patients who coped well were appropriately frightened by the damage to their eyes but willing to make the necessary adjustments. They trusted in God, were optimistic about the outcome of the surgery, and confident of their ability to redefine their lives if the operation was not a success. They were open and friendly, appeared to be at home with themselves, took care of themselves and graciously accepted the help of others. Correlations between acceptance level and speed of healing were very high. According to the chaplain who did this study, faith was an important resource in coping with this situation:

> If patients used their faith as a source of strength to face reality
> and deal with it constructively, they were rapid healers. If they

used their faith to hide from reality, or to manipulate or force God's hand, they were slow healers. Those who could accept their detachment, as part of the bad that befalls us along with the good in life, healed well. Those who felt that their detachment was a foul blow, and God a monster for permitting it to happen, healed poorly, if they healed at all.[5]

A sense of coherence is rarely maintained without social support. A view of the world becomes comprehensible through what Peter Berger calls plausibility structures, structures which provide consistent reinforcement to people who share the same worldview. A strong support system also makes the world more manageable. Meaningfulness, the third factor in a sense of coherence, rarely exists apart from participation in a community of conviction.

A wide variety of studies indicates that people with strong social support are less susceptible to disease and death than those who are isolated. Men in Japan have one-fifth the number of heart attacks of U.S. men. Those who move to the United States and adopt a Western pattern of social relationships move up to the norm in this country. The Japanese-Americans who maintain traditions and community ties like those of their homeland do not show the same rate of increase in heart attacks, and the difference is not related to diet, exercise, smoking, or any other variables related to health maintenance. A group of thirty elderly people in retirement homes showed increased immune competence after being visited three times a week for a month. In a study of 256 healthy elderly people, those with confiding relationships had significantly higher indices of immune function and lower serum cholesterol levels. In the year following a heart attack, pet owners have one-fifth the death rate of those who are petless.

Social support is related to good health in those who provide the support as well as in those who receive it. This may be one reason why there is such an emphasis in most religions upon caring for others. Doing so is helpful to the donor as well as to the

5. Robert Reeves, "Healing and Salvation: A Clinical View," in *Healing and Religious Faith*, ed. Claude Frazier (Philadelphia: United Church Press, 1974), p. 100.

entire community. When college students were shown a film of Mother Teresa tending to the sick and dying poor of Calcutta, their immune functioning immediately increased and remained elevated one hour later. The effect occurred even in people who reported consciously disliking Mother Teresa. A number of studies indicate that people with "altruistic egoism" live longer and healthier lives than those who are concerned only about their own health and welfare. Even attending to a pet or a plant seems to have health benefits. This is not intended as an argument for increased service to humanity, if for no other reason than care for others would likely lose its health value if done for reasons other than altruism.

Touch can be singled out as one aspect of caring and nurturing relationships that is particularly important for health and healing. Most of us know from our own experience how important touch is, especially when we are ill. Touch by a caregiver or a friend is rarely considered invasive in a hospital setting, perhaps because we feel isolated and disconnected in this impersonal world. A friend of mine once told me about preparing for his surgery by imagining family and friends surrounding the surgical table, each with a hand on his body. Touch communicates connectedness, care, loving support, and nurture in a way that words cannot. Many of the healing stories of Jesus tell us that he touched those whom he healed. An ancient Christian ritual of touching is the "laying on of hands," which is once again being used regularly in healing services.

The importance of touch for healing was shown in a study that was not designed for that purpose. A group of investigators at Ohio State University were studying the effects of a diet high in fat and cholesterol on rabbits. At the end of a prescribed period, the rabbits were killed and their arteries were examined for evidence of atherosclerosis, a condition in which cholesterol forms deposits in the arteries. While the results of the study were not unexpected, the investigators were puzzled when one group of test rabbits demonstrated a cholesterol build-up that was 60 percent less than that of the overall group. Upon further investigation, it was discovered that the rabbits who were less affected were those who were fed and cared for by an attendant who regularly took them from their cages and petted them while he talked to them. The experiment was repeated two more times in order to test for this variable, and the results were the same each time.

Touch evokes trust, as a recent experiment demonstrates. Money was left in a phone booth to be found by the next caller. The experimenter approached, said the money was his, and asked if he could have it back. The money was seldom returned unless the experimenter touched the person while talking. It may be that touch forms a bond of trust that resonates with our earliest memories of being held. Without such holding, children can literally die or be psychologically maimed for life. Touching and trusting are both vital for health and healing.

Having a sense of coherence is important for achieving and maintaining wellness, while lack of control and the absence of meaning foster a sense of helplessness that undermines health. At least this much seems clear from the studies cited above. This sense of coherence is a faith factor in healing in much the same way as the placebo effect, and we will devote the remaining portion of this chapter to its analysis and application.

Finding a Broader Frame of Reference Than Case History

If feelings of helplessness contribute to illness and if a sense of coherence contributes to health, then the need to expand the medical perspective beyond a narrow focus on case histories is clear. As I have suggested from the beginning, the broader frame of reference is the person who is ill. With the acknowledgment of that broader frame of reference comes the realization that the traditional method of case history is no longer adequate.

The science of medicine equips physicians to treat organic disease, the symptoms of which are diagnosed by means of case history and eliminated by means of surgery and/or medication. The common complaint of patients that their physician does not listen to them is true in relation to the story of the illness but not in relation to the symptoms of disease. The physician listens carefully for what he or she is trained to detect, symptoms of an organic disease which can be reversed by appropriate intervention. The limitations of this approach are indicated by Eric Cassell:

> Our science is based on the measurement of the finite, the rendering of the phenomena into numbers. It is common to confuse the question we are asking with the method we use to get the answer. Yet the method used determines the nature of the answer. If we were asked to describe a rose and we were given only a ruler to do it, the picture of the rose that emerged would be solely in terms of inches. The picture would be true but incomplete. If a ruler were our only way of describing things, we would not know that the picture was incomplete. Our knowledge of the universe is a function of our technology, and technology is a function of our philosophical view of the universe.
>
> The three searches that pervade the history of medicine—*what, why, what can we do about it*—are universal. But illness is a special phenomenon. It has both objective and personal aspects, and thus the questions have both an objective and a personal meaning. The search for definitions of illness was essential to provide a basis for any further inquiry, but it is clear to anybody who has ever been ill that the ontological definitions of disease that have emerged from our history in terms of structural and chemical change and that leave out the individual are an incomplete picture of illness. The complete picture would involve other, more personal phenomena.[6]

The title of Cassell's book, *The Healer's Art*, is indicative of his view that the art of medicine is as important as the science. Practicing the art of medicine means relating to the person who is ill as well as treating the organic disease. "Illness," as we have been using the term, denotes the subjective experience of the person who is sick. As Cassell puts it, "illness" stands for what a person feels when he or she goes to the doctor, and "disease" for what he or she has on the way home from the doctor's office. That is both gain and loss, knowing more and knowing less. What is easily lost, because it is discounted, is the meaning of the subjective experience.

6. Eric J. Cassell, *The Healer's Art* (Cambridge, Mass: MIT Press, 1976), p. 64.

When the subjective experience of illness becomes extended, as in chronic conditions, or catastrophic, as in the loss of a limb, it can be described as disruption of self; it is an experience of disintegration in a self that ought to feel whole or complete. Have you ever had the experience of your body being something foreign, a nonself that is unmanageable? Oliver Sacks gives us a good example of this sense of self-disruption in his book *A Leg to Stand On*.[7] After suffering extensive nerve damage in his leg as a result of a fall, Sacks lost any sense that his leg was attached to his body. More than a functional disturbance that comes with a feeling of numbness or inability to move the leg, this experience was nothing less than an "ontological assault" affecting his very being as an integrated whole.

In his masterful short story entitled "The Metamorphosis,"[8] Franz Kafka provides us with an excellent metaphor for capturing the sense of self-disruption that so often accompanies the experience of catastrophic illness. Grego Samsa wakes up one morning to discover that he has turned into a giant insect. The story details his sufferings and eventual death in this state and his family's reactions to his situation. Lying on his back with six stubby legs flailing in the air, when he tries to get up, he can not maneuver his unwieldy body. Eventually he learns how to use his body and even enjoys climbing the walls and ceiling. But he never gets out of the room and is treated by his family at first with disbelief and disgust, then dutifully, then with resentment, and finally as a foreign presence to which they owe no obligations. The analogy between the self-transformation that takes place in catastrophic illness and metamorphosis into an insect may be overdrawn, but there is no denying how deeply our sense of self is rooted in the body and how difficult it is to maintain a sense of coherence when there are radical changes in the body.

The value of a metaphor for the experience of self-disruption in illness is in the meaning that it gives to illness. The danger is

7. Oliver Sacks, *A Leg to Stand On* (New York: Summit Books, 1984).
8. Franz Kafka, "The Metamorphosis," in *The Basic Kafka* (New York: Pocket Books, 1979).

that the metaphor may be destructive. Susan Sontag has shown the destructive consequences of giving metaphorical meaning to illnesses such as cancer and AIDS, meaning that is invariably moralistic.[9] People project meanings onto these diseases which stereotype and condemn the victims to suffering beyond the physical burden which the disease brings. Cancer is regarded with irrational revulsion, as a diminution of self. Cancer is perceived as dark and menacing, self-destructive (generated by one's own cells and related to self-hate), and invariably resulting in a death that is painful and slow. AIDS is perceived as a generic rebuke to life and hope, and its metaphoric meanings are much harsher and more judgmental than those associated with cancer. Because most of the victims of this illness are members of a misunderstood minority, the perception of the disease is filtered through the fear and abhorrence of what some people regard as patently evil.

So giving meaning to illness is not always a plus for the person who is ill. Indeed, Sontag argues, "My point is that illness is *not* a metaphor, and that the most truthful way of regarding illness— and the healthiest way of being ill—is one most purified of, most resistant to, metaphoric thinking."[10] To take this advice would be to follow the course of medical science and disregard the element of subjectivity. We cannot help giving disease a meaning. Metaphors, symbols, and images can be used in both constructive and destructive ways. Our task is to construct metaphors and meaning maps that alleviate suffering rather than contribute to it. We have the resources to do that through the stories we tell, especially the master story found in every religion.

For all the reasons listed above, the meaning of illness and health must be broader than the traditional biomedical definitions. Thus physical illness must be described as both a breakdown in the smooth and well-ordered functioning of biological mechanisms and a disruption of the self and its sense of coher-

9. Susan Sontag, *AIDS and Its Metaphors* (New York: Farrar, Straus & Giroux, 1988).
10. Susan Sontag, *Illness as Metaphor* (New York: Farrar, Straus & Giroux, 1978), p. 3.

ence, each intimately related to the other. The need for holistic definitions is even more obvious in the case of health, which biomedicine defines as the absence of any symptoms of disease. A broader, more positive definition is internal coherence of body and self experienced as a feeling of ease, internal harmony, and balance. To be healthy is to have an intimate and free-flowing connectedness to body, others, and God. Cassell captures this meaning in the following description:

> When you run you are not supposed to look at your feet; it gets in the way of running. When you drive you just look where you want to go and the car obeys. If you have to concentrate on how to drive, you are not a driver yet. So it is with all the functions of life: we just do without an awareness of doing. Life is function. Health, at least in part, incorporates the ability of the self to soar, allied with, but unhampered by and unaware of, the confines of the body—unaware at least consciously, for somewhere within there must be, in true health, a unity between self and body. The healthy have confidence in themselves and in their bodies, a confidence built on experience and fed by the sense of invulnerability.[11]

The meaning of health is manifested most clearly when it is recovered after an incapacitating illness. Even recovery from a minor illness such as the flu can bring a feeling of ease and sense of soaring, but in *Awakenings* Oliver Sacks tells the stories of the truly remarkable recoveries of patients who had been afflicted with extreme forms of Parkinsonism.[12] Treated with L-DOPA, a new wonder drug in the 1960s, many of these patients who had been locked inside their bodies (severely limited in speech and mobility) for over twenty years regained full function of their physical powers within days, only to lose it again within days. Sacks comments on the experience of one patient who had a full but brief recovery:

> "It's a very sweet feeling," he said (during his own so-brief awakening), "very sweet and easy and peaceful. I am grateful to each moment for being itself . . . I feel so contented, like I'm at home at last after a long hard journey. Just as warm and peaceful as a cat

11. Cassell, *The Healer's Art*, p. 125.
12. Oliver Sacks, *Awakenings* (New York: E. P. Dutton, 1983).

by the fire." And this was exactly how he *looked* at that moment:
> . . . Like a cat asleep on a chair, at peace, in peace,
> and at one with the master of the house, with the mistress,
> at home, at home in the house of the living,
> sleeping on the hearth, and yawning before the fire.
> Sleeping on the hearth of the living world
> yawning at home before the fire of life
> feeling the presence of the living God
> like a great reassurance
> a deep calm in the heart
> a presence
> as of the master sitting at the board
> in his own and greater being
> in the house of life.

—D. H. Lawrence[13]

A Narrative Structure
for Giving Meaning to Illness

There is a small core of medical authors who are encouraging their colleagues to expand their case histories of disease management to include stories of illness. The clinical biographies in Sacks' *Awakenings* are good examples of how a narrative structure can give meaning to illness. Technical scientific language is used to describe the organic malfunctions, but these technical descriptions are set within narrative accounts that reveal the personal meaning of illness and the variety of ways that individuals cope with the changes that an experience of illness brings.

Howard Brody says that "we are, in an important sense, the stories of our lives. How sickness affects us depends on how sickness alters those stories. Both sick persons and physicians make the experience of sickness more meaningful (thereby reducing suffering) by placing it within the context of a meaningful story." Thus "every medical history should include a description of what the illness means to the patient —what the patient thinks has caused it, what he thinks will happen to him in the future as a result, and what he thinks the best treatment ought to be." Only after listening carefully to the patient's way of organiz-

13. Ibid., pp. 215f.

ing and giving meaning to events should a physician bring all available scientific knowledge to bear upon the story and give back to the patient a revised, medicalized, and professionalized version of the story of the illness. "It may reasonably be hypothesized that the placebo effect, well known to be ubiquitous in medicine, works precisely by way of this meaning route—a story that makes sense, implies enhanced social support and caring, and tends to lead toward mastery and control of the illness will maximize the perceived (and objective) relief of the sickness episode."[14]

When a disease is well understood, a doctor's explanation restores a sense of coherence. He or she may say, "You have a hiatus hernia, which means that a part of your stomach has been pushed up into the hole of the diaphragm through which the esophagus passes to join the stomach; and while this may cause you some discomfort, it is easy to take care of and will do you no harm."[15] Such an explanation is not sufficient if the trouble is something that medicine cannot do anything about, something which will result either in death or long-term chronic illness. In such cases a different kind of explanation is needed to give meaning to the story of illness. A sensitive doctor will be attentive to the need for deeper dimensions of meaning in such cases and either help patients discern that larger framework of meaning or refer them to chaplains or others who are trained to do so.

Physicians should be trained to listen carefully to the stories their patients tell and to engage them in meaningful conversation that will help to protect and restore the sense of coherence which enables them to live with meaning and purpose. They should listen especially to the religious stories people tell when there is nothing within biomedicine that will correct the destructive course that an illness is taking. At such times only a "big-enough" story will be able to restore and possibly transform the sense of coherence which the self needs, even when and especially when sickness cannot be cured.

14. Brody, *Stories of Sickness*, pp. 182, 184, 185.
15. Cassell, *The Healer's Art*, p. 129.

The illness narratives of John Donne and Cornelius Ryan demonstrate the importance of stories for understanding the meaning of illness. Donne's *Devotions upon Emergent Occasions* must be read within the context of seventeenth-century culture, when serious illness meant that one took to bed, waited for the disease to reach its climax, endured the critical days, and patiently endured a lengthy period of convalescence.[16] The passivity with which the patient was expected to accept the will of God in the course of the disease stands in striking contrast to the description of Cornelius Ryan in *A Private Battle*,[17] where the model is the war hero who fights valiantly to the end against great odds.

Donne sees a close connection between the travail of the body and the travail of the soul, and Ryan between illness and war. For Donne religion provides a uniform model that explains the meaning of illness and the way to experience it. Ryan uses the metaphor of battle to understand the meaning of cancer, perceived by him and many in our culture as an alien intruder and silent destroyer. For Donne everything that happens to his body in the course of his illness has a counterpart in the life of his soul. His is a sacramental view of illness and healing. For Ryan illness has no meaning other than that of evil—cancer with the face of a mass murderer. Ryan, a famous journalist and historian of World War II, became ill with cancer while he was researching and writing *A Bridge Too Far*, an epic account of a famous battle toward the end of the war. His story, as told by himself and his wife in *A Private Battle*, is full of stoic courage as he fought to complete this project. Donne uses Christian metaphors and images to find meaning and comfort in his illness, over which he had no more control than Ryan.

The stories of Ryan and Donne show the human need and capacity to transcend illness with the aid of metaphor and myth. I personally find the account of Donne more compelling, but that

16. A. Hawkins, "Two Pathographies: A Study in Illness and Literature," *The Journal of Medicine and Philosophy* 9, no. 3 (Aug. 1984): 231–52.
17. Cornelius Ryan, *A Bridge Too Far* (New York: Simon & Schuster, 1974).

is because I share with him the larger story that brought meaning to his illness.

What one is struggling to preserve when ill is not just life but one's world. The more disruptive the illness, the more likely will this be the case. At one point the patient in Alexander R. Luria's *The Man with a Shattered World* says, "Why doesn't my memory function, my sight return? ... It's depressing, having to start all over and make sense out of a world you've lost because of injury and illness, to get these bits and pieces to add up to a coherent whole." To which Sacks comments, "A *world* is lost or broken or unmade, reduced to bits and pieces, to chaos—and it is a *world*, no less, that must be remade."[18] Both the body and the self struggle to bring some order, some organization to the threatening chaos of illness. The most that the body can achieve is some semblance of the coherence that characterizes health, but the self has the capacity to construct a new world, a transcendent order that is more stable and satisfying than anything known before. Sickness destroys this capacity only in extreme cases, such as brain damage so extensive that a person cannot remember anything for more than a few minutes.

It is this capacity to construct a world of meaning in the form of a story that makes us human and accounts for our spiritual development. I know who I am by remembering and telling my story. There may be a radical disruption in my sense of coherence, so much so that I feel like a different person, but I am still the same person in that it remains the story of my life. And even though I feel like a different person, I am still connected to earlier experience by means of memory and to future experience by means of anticipation. Memory and anticipation are the distinctively human capacities needed in the making of meaning and the constructing of stories.

That we can remember and anticipate is both a curse and a blessing. So terror-filled can memories and anticipations be that some choose unconsciously to construct an imaginary story

18. Oliver Sacks, "Clinical Tales," in *Literature and Medicine*, vol. 5, ed. Joanne Trautmann Banks (Baltimore: Johns Hopkins University Press, 1986), p. 18.

within a psychotic world rather than face the overwhelming fears that make living in the real world seem completely untenable. Yet even here the need for story as a way of finding meaning remains central, however illusory and ephemeral the story may be.

The need for stories to bring meaning to illness is particularly strong among those who are chronically ill. I teach a course entitled "Spiritual Needs and Health Care," and one of the requirements of the course is that students interview someone who is disabled or chronically ill. The reports the students bring back are testimonials to the power of stories in bringing meaning to illness. Though suffering can embitter those who are touched by it, in the vast majority of cases suffering serves as a catalyst, transforming persons who are ill into powerful witnesses to the meaning of life. Their personal history forces them into a dialogue with suffering, usually in God's presence. They are graced with the capacity to see in their stories the presence and the power of God suffering with them through Christ, and from this comes comfort and courage. Telling such stories is "breaking open the hidden holy that dwells in our experience," as Sue Kidd puts it.[19] The key point here is that meaning is discovered in events that could only be described as depressing and unholy (lacking wholeness) from an objective (medical) point of view.

The need for meaning in the story of a person's life remains strong even when the story is coming to an end. It may take the form of living on through one's children or nation. It may take the form of leaving a heritage such as a work of art. It may take the form of hope in life after death, as in the Christian story. Our current preoccupation with health to the point of idolatry is fueled, at least in part, by the need for a story that will not end. In a secular culture that has few enduring values and holds little hope for life after death, frenetic efforts to maintain health may be the current expression of a yearning for immortality.

A narrative structure for giving meaning to illness is needed in order to fully include the faith factor in healing. The rational,

19. Sue Kidd, "The Story-Shaped Life," *Weavings* 4 (Jan./Feb. 1989).

scientific, and objective reporting in a case history has nothing of the intuitive, imaginative, and dramatic dimensions which inform story. I require nursing and pre-med students to listen carefully to the stories of people who have found meaning through their encounters with suffering, because the quality of their caregiving is dependent on their ability and willingness to listen to the stories that people tell them. What a blessing for patients it would be if every medical professional conducted an in-depth interview of a handicapped or chronically ill person once a year and discussed it with someone who is trained to discern spiritual needs in the stories that people tell.

Overworked nurses and physicians will quickly tell you that they do not have time to listen to the stories of individual patients. End of discussion. Or is it? Perhaps this issue needs to be at the beginning of a discussion between a person and his or her prospective physician. Case history without soul history excludes faith as a relevant factor in healing when it excludes stories that reveal the meaning of illness. Saying that there is not time for such matters is saying that faith is peripheral and not all that important, and that is worth discussing.

What kind of stories are important for discerning the meaning of your illness and the kind of treatment that is appropriate for you? Stories about who you are, where you have come from, and where you are going. In other words, stories about your identity. How does a particular illness affect your self-understanding and feelings of self-worth? That depends on the illness, of course, but it also depends on the fund of stories from which you can draw to give meaning to this illness, set it within a larger frame of reference, and find hope in a future that may be full of dark shadows. Without discounting the value of getting an objective assessment of the disease from a competent physician, it is even more valuable to understand how this illness fits within the story of your life.

Clifford Geertz, well known as an analyst of culture, describes human beings as animals suspended in webs of significance that they themselves spin. Those webs are the stories that people tell, and their analysis is not a science in search of law but an interpretation in search of meaning. That is why medicine is an art as well as a science. Our lives are story-shaped, and the important task of ordering the impending chaos of a disrupted world into a cosmos of meaning is the work of an artist. That is a relational task, of course, and the story that emerges from it is the product of the relationship between physician and patient. The physician is often in a position to offer the reassuring word that the illness has a name and that medicine is equipped to reverse its course. But sometimes illness has no name and a physician no equipment to reverse its course. At that point, soul care is more important than physical care and stories about meaning more important than stories about physical care.

Communities are the chief depositories of stories about meaning, stories that undergird our identity and assure us of historical continuity. The Christian community has many stories about illness and healing, most of them centered around the ministry of Jesus, who has often been called the Great Physician. We turn our attention now to how Christians frame their stories of illness and healing. Nobody experiences illness in a vacuum, without faith, without some way of making sense out of what is happening. The Christian community is not the only one with stories of healing and a rich tradition for interpreting the meaning of illness and healing, but I am assuming that the majority of those who will read this book share that tradition or are familiar enough with it to see how important such a tradition is for transforming the seeming chaos of self-disruption into a meaningful story full of promise and hope.

Framing Stories of Illness and Healing
as a Christian

Case history and soul history are two traditional methods for generating stories of illness, and I have been suggesting that a combination of the two is needed for the stories to be complete and for the care provided to be adequate. The faith factor in story making is "meaning," and it is this factor that we are particularly concerned with in this section. What does this illness mean for my body, for my mind, for my world, for my life plan, for my self-respect, for my continuing identity?

There are both penultimate and ultimate answers to those questions. For Christians, the ultimate answers come from the story of God's saving acts in history. The broad sweep of this story can be depicted as a drama in four acts. The first act is the creation of the world, and the Garden of Eden is the symbol of its goodness. Here we find the biblical norms of health and wholeness not in definitions but in images of a world that God calls good and in stories of people who were called to nurture the world and bring it to fulfillment. The second act is the story of the fall into sin and its consequences for all of humanity, for all of the world. The deepest meanings of illness are related to this story, including the meaning of death. It is a story seemingly without end, and the images which it generates are tolerable only because the third act of this drama promises deliverance from the pit of self-destruction which humanity digs deeper and deeper. The third act is the story of God's restoration of the created order. It is a story of healing which Scripture records in both Old and New Testament, a story which reaches its climax in the death and resurrection of Christ. In this story are to be found the Christian's deepest meanings of healing and health, and from it emerge images of hope and renewal. The last act of the drama is the complete and total realization of the wholeness which God had intended from the beginning. This story is not a repetition of the Garden of Eden, but rather the fulfillment of a new creation which is richer and fuller because of the struggle that has preceded it.

This is the master story for Christians, the most comprehensive frame of reference for understanding the meaning of illness and healing. It is this story which undergirds and contextualizes the sense of coherence that Christians use to frame the narrative structure of illness and healing in their lives. It is not a story Christians create when they become ill. It is the story of their lives since baptism, a story to which they turn for meaning when illness strikes. And the more tragic the illness and the longer its duration, the more deeply they dip into the wellsprings of this story for strength, for healing, and for continuing identity. There is only one master story for Christians, but there is an infinite variety of ways in which that story intersects with the lives of individual Christians. The creativity in story-telling resides in that intersection. The sweeping generalizations about the meaning of illness and healing in the Old and New Testaments which follow should in no way be regarded as the only way in which that story can be interpreted. My intention is to provide the reader with an occasion to find his or her point of intersection with that master story.

The Meaning of Illness and Healing in the Old Testament

There are several different strands of meaning that come from Old Testament stories and reflections on the meaning of illness. Above all, illness is regarded as punishment and healing as a reward for righteous living. That theme is particularly striking in the Psalms, many of which were written in periods of illness, but it runs throughout the Old Testament. Though this strand of meaning is muted in the New Testament, it is never far from the consciousness of Christians, who are often quick to assume that they have done something to deserve the illness which has befallen them.

The attitude of getting what one deserves in illness, health, and healing is most prominent today among advocates of the wellness movement and New Age self-healing. The logic is simple. Since we are responsible for our health, we deserve the illness which comes as a consequence of failure to take care of ourself. And since we have the capacity to heal ourself, there must be something wrong with our attitude or faith if we do not improve. Such moralism is merely annoying in health promotion, but it becomes destructive when applied to those who are ill, many of whom are made to feel guilty because their attitude is not upbeat enough, their faith not strong enough, or their imagery not positive enough.

A second strand of meaning in the Old Testament is the story of Job, who struggles mightily for meaning but finally realizes that his illness is a mystery that can be fathomed ultimately only by the mind of God. In his effort to understand the "why" of his illness, Job rejects his counselors' arguments for the traditional view that we get what we deserve when it comes to illness and health. Maintaining his integrity throughout the narrative, Job insists on pursuing the issue of the injustice of his suffering to the highest court available and, wonder of wonders, Yahweh appears to Job out of the whirlwind. But it is Job who is questioned rather than Yahweh, and Job acknowledges that illness is a mystery that can be fully known only by God.

This strand of meaning has been of great comfort to Christians through the centuries. Understanding illness as mystery does not mean that we are without rational structures for comprehending its meaning, both medical and nonmedical; it means only that those structures are limited and ultimately inadequate for grasping the full meaning of this phenomenon. The story of Job is a reminder to Christians that this is true also for the best of their explanations, and that this in no way invalidates the gospel promise that "all things work together for good to those who love God" (Rom. 8:28). Chaos surrounds Job on every side, but never does he doubt the power of God to control the destiny of the cosmos and the fate of individuals within it.

The third strand of meaning in the Old Testament is that the suffering in illness can be redemptive. In Isaiah's depiction of the servant who suffers, we hear intimations of the redemptive suffering of Christ. Matthew understood it that way when he used the image of the suffering servant in a commentary on the healings of Jesus: "This was to fulfil what was spoken by the prophet Isaiah, 'He took our infirmities and bore our diseases'" (Matt. 8:17). Healings would accompany the new age of the Messiah, and both Jesus and his followers interpret his healings as signs of the coming of the kingdom of God.

The Meaning of Illness and Healing in the New Testament

For Christians the story of Jesus is the definitive frame of reference for the narrative structure of illness and healing in their personal and communal lives. In Jesus the promise of healing is nothing less than "the mending of creation," as Krister Stendahl once put it. One must begin with that as the largest frame of reference for meaning in order not to move too quickly to questions about what is happening to "little me," as if that were what the whole drama of salvation was all about. The healings of Jesus were signs of the in-breaking power of the Kingdom of God and the dethroning of powers of evil. The ultimate sign of healing, so understood, is the cross of Christ. The resurrection that follows completes the mending of creation by revealing the consequences of Jesus' healing sacrifice, including the gift of healing.

The death/resurrection of Christ, seen as a single event, is at the very center of the narrative structure of illness and healing for Christians. What we learn from this story is that health is not an end in itself, as it is so often represented in recent literature on health and healing. The story of Jesus contrasts sharply with the story of the modern "healthy" person. Jesus is the wounded healer, dying that others might live. How different is that image from the picture of physical vitality, positive attitude, and social support that is held up as the ideal of health in most of the self-help literature. In the story of Jesus there is no wholeness apart from the care of others, and the symbol of the cross is an invitation to Christians to use their health in a manner similar to Jesus.

If we construct our stories of illness in the shadow of the cross, then suffering can be redemptive and transforming. That is especially true when we grow into sensitive awareness of the suffering of others, not only people we know but also those far removed from us: neglected children, the homeless, the hungry. That is what Henri Nouwen means by a wounded healer, whose "service will not be perceived as authentic unless it comes from a heart wounded by the suffering about which he speaks."[20]

Earlier in my life I thought only voluntary suffering was a sacrament of healing in the sense that one could see the healing Christ in it. But then I came to know an elderly woman who was confined to bed with a chronic illness that brought suffering into

20. Henri Nouwen, *The Wounded Healer* (Garden City, N.Y.: Doubleday & Co., 1972), p. xiv.

her life that was anything but voluntary. She had but one talent—faithful, long-suffering endurance—to use in coping with this frightful burden. I came to see her life as cruciform, and she became for me a powerful witness to the meaning that Christ brings to an apparently meaningless life. Those who suffer, as well as those who are in good health, can become wounded healers when the narrative structure of their lives bears the imprint of the death/resurrection of Christ.

Only after we have taken with full seriousness the meaning of the cross for our stories of illness and healing can we give expression to the promise of continued life and perfect health in the resurrection. The promise of good enough if not perfect health is what fuels the health care movement and gives to physicians their almost god-like authority. Yet the dramatic successes of medicine always run out at some point, and the healthiest of lives come inexorably to a close. Nothing is more sure. That we are mortal creatures who have a beginning and an end like every other living organism is no more extraordinary than anything else in the wonderful world of nature. But the mortal creature that is human contains a self that feels ageless and yearns for immortality. The quest for immortality is an expression of our genuine humanity, quite apart from the question about whether mortality is or is not built into a good and ordered creation. The promise of the resurrection meets the spiritual need for historical continuity and is the source of hope which sustains Christians in their dying and their grieving of loved ones.

The stories of healing in the Gospels are important but are not of ultimate importance for understanding the stories of illness and healing in the lives of Christians. Physical healing, whether done by medical or spiritual means, is only temporary. Even as dramatic a healing as that of Lazarus did not preclude a second coming of illness and death in what remained of the story of his life. In spite of these qualifications, the healings of Jesus are the centerpiece of his ministry on earth and a model for the church's healing ministry. Even a cursory reading of those stories makes it clear that healing (including physical healing) is the will of God. Jesus did not heal everybody he met, but it would be hard to imagine Jesus refusing a request for healing because he did not consider it to be God's will for this person. The example of Jesus makes it crystal clear that soul healing alone is a narrow and abridged version of the church's mission.

What does it mean for us that Jesus healed people of physical diseases? At the very least it means that physical healing and health ought to receive as much attention from us as they did from Jesus, though only in the context of spiritual healing and health. Christians should support medicine's recent interest in faith, because faith is as important a factor in healing as medication. At the same time Christians need to rediscover their rich tradition of physical healing in light of what we have come to know about the close connection between spiritual and physical functioning. We are far from the truth of the gospel when we pit the healing stories of Jesus against modern medical stories of healing, even when we say both/and rather than either/or. The real question is how these two great traditions of healing can each respond more effectively to the "wholeness hunger" of those in need of care.

This leads to the second source of meaning in the healing stories of Jesus—whole person healing. Nobody argues with this today, even in medicine, but the healing stories of Jesus provide a very clear perspective for seeing the interconnections between physical and spiritual healing. The division between soul and body, so deeply embedded in our way of thinking, is simply absent in these stories. The healing of the paralytic (Mark 2:1-2) is a good example. Jesus forgives when you expect him to heal and heals when you expect him to forgive; healing and forgiving are simply two aspects of a larger whole. To people who have solidified a useful distinction between soul and body into an impenetrable boundary, this is confusing. Fortunately, there has been a greater emphasis recently on whole person care in both medicine and religion.

A third source of meaning in the healings of Jesus is the faith factor in healing. Though faith is not a necessary condition for healing in the ministry of Jesus, at least judging by the limited number of times it is mentioned, everything that Jesus said and did invited expectant trust from those who were in need of healing. Sometimes faith is clearly a factor, as when Jesus says to the woman who touched his garment, "Daughter, your faith has made you well" (Mark 5:34). At other times it is the faith of others that is mentioned (Mark 2:5) or faith that comes only after the healing (Luke 17:15). The faith factor that medicine has discovered in the placebo effect is illustrated in the Gospels and interpreted in relation to God.

At the very least the faith factor in the healing stories of Jesus rules out the kind of passive role that we often assume in a healing relationship, whether it be with a physician or God. We expect the doctor or God to do something *to* us to make us well. We are like clay in the potter's hands. Such passivity and total dependence have been reinforced by both medicine and religion. It is the physician who prescribes the medication and/or surgery that will make us physically well, and it is God by grace alone who makes us spiritually well and, when God wills it, also physically well. Taken to its logical conclusion, this negates one's participation in healing, physical or spiritual. Not so, according to the evidence we have assembled in these last two chapters; faith is an important factor in healing when healing is defined as interactional rather than as something a healer does to a person who is ill.

Faith has always been closely linked to healing in the Christian tradition. Thus it is strange, and no small irony, that the faith factor in healing is regarded as negatively in the church as it is in medicine, though for a different reason. Put it to a personal test. Would you go to a faith healer? If not, why not? The checkered history of faith healing has made many Christians as skeptical as scientists of the fraudulent claims so often made by those who claim to be instruments of God. Such suspicion makes it more difficult to get a fair hearing for the legitimate claim that faith plays a prominent role in healing, wherever and however it occurs.

Framing My Stories of Illness

I conclude this chapter where I began, by noting the importance of a comprehensive framework of meaning for stories of illness, healing, and health. As humans we cannot live without stories. The only question is how to frame them. The biblical drama of salvation provides the framework for Christians, and this chapter suggests some of what that means for individual stories of illness and healing. Clinical biographies that combine case history and soul history offer our best hope for framing stories that are true to the empirical facts and the deepest meanings of human existence. I have argued that medical professionals have a responsibility to listen more attentively to the stories of illness that people tell, but the responsibility for framing the story belongs to each individual person. How then should Christians frame their stories if the biblical drama of salvation is the master story that they use for understanding illness and healing in their lives?

The answer to that question has varied considerably in different historical eras and among different Christian groups. The holistic healing so characteristic of the ministry of Jesus became increasingly narrow in the centuries following his death. Anointing the sick for purposes of healing (James 5) became a rite for preparing the soul for its departure from the body. Only the fate of the soul was important in the story of a person's life.

There is no frame of reference for understanding stories of physical illness if the gospel is defined exclusively in terms of the salvation of the soul. At best, the fate of those who are ill is determined by the laws of nature within the order of creation. Stories of illness become stories of bodies without souls—case histories, histories of diseases, and treatment procedures without people.

A rereading of the biblical drama of salvation supplies us with a new set of meanings for framing our stories of wellness, illness, and healing. Though each person's story is unique, we can make some broad applications from this master story to the stories of our lives. As I do this, I will pose questions that will help you to apply those meanings more directly to your own life.

First, there are stories of wellness in the biblical drama of salvation. From the earliest stories of the Garden of Eden, health is depicted as a gift that God intends for every living creature. Adam, representative of all humanity, was given "dominion" over the entire created order, but with a steward's responsibility to nurture and sustain this gift of life in all of creation. This commissioning of humanity gives us not the rule of a despot over property to dispose of as we choose but the role of a priest to mediate God's gracious caretaking. There is no wellness apart from such a caretaking role, even though such care might entail a sacrifice of our good health.

What are the wellness stories that come to mind as you reflect on your personal history? When did your world seem most "together" and you most fully the kind of person that God intended you to be? Were there many such periods and how long did they last? How have you used or perhaps abused your wellness? How does the care of others fit into the story of your life? Name three sacrifices that you have made that have posed a threat to your health and well-being. Would you say that you are well at this point in your life? What does that wellness mean to you and how do you intend to use it in the present chapter of your life?

As important as our stories of wellness are, it is the stories of illness and healing that are the most dramatic and command the most attention. We have spoken at length about such stories in this chapter and about the need for placing them within an ultimate frame of reference, which for Christians is the drama of God's mending of the whole creation. It is from this master story that Christians can draw the meanings to frame their stories of illness and healing.

We are ever in danger of losing our groundedness in this master story. There are so many secular forces that subtly erode the meanings in the story of our salvation and substitute alternative ways of salvation to those we find in the church. We need to hear in a new way the biblical stories of healing that provide the images and symbols for the framing of our own stories of illness and healing. We also need the drama to be enacted through healing liturgies. And we need programs to train lay people as healers, such as the Stephen Ministries, a transdenominational, international caring ministry organization founded by Kenneth Haugk and based in St. Louis, Missouri. We need institutional structures such as holistic health centers and parish nurse programs to provide the very best context for linking case history to soul history. Finally, we need spiritual direction and pastoral counseling to help us reflect on our life journey.

What are the stories of illness that come to your mind when you reflect on your personal history? Remember those occasions when you felt most strongly a sense of impending chaos from a serious physical illness or some other crisis that carried with it the threat of self-disruption. Where did you turn for help? What was it that gave you hope? Was faith a factor in your healing or in coping with a condition for which there was no healing? If so, how? Either now or at some later date, write a full and detailed account of a story of illness in your life. The more recent, the better. Look for themes in the story, for a sequence of events that suggests a pattern, and for the personal style of coping that characterizes your way of being in the world. You will find this a useful reflection exercise after any episode of illness. At no other time in our lives are we likely to be as sensitive to questions of meaning as during periods of illness.

Finally, there are stories of dying. It is not likely that you will know about this through personal experience, though perhaps a physical illness or accident brought you to the brink of death. But you are likely to have been a participant in the dying of a parent, grandparent, or someone else you knew well. And probably you have reflected on your own dying in anticipation of an event that you know will be part of your life.[21] Larry Churchill makes a strong argument for the moral primacy of stories over stages in the human experience of dying. The advantage of story over stage is that "the interpretation of the meaning of events is provided by the dying person. Only the dying person can narrate or tell the story, because only he or she knows how the story goes."[22] And how it ends. Nowhere is the need for a larger framework of meaning more obvious than with the dying. All of

21. For a wide variety of guided imagery exercises that are designed to help people anticipate their own dying, see Thomas A. Droege, *Guided Grief Imagery* (Mahwah, N.J.: Paulist Press, 1987).

22. Larry R. Churchill, "The Human Experience of Dying: The Moral Primacy of Stories over Stages," *Soundings* 52 (1983): 29.

us need to be able to chart our own course for this last event in the story of our lives.

How close have you come to death? What events in your life have prompted you to think about your own dying? Were you able to do that with relative ease or did you discover considerable resistance within yourself? What are the resources of faith that you draw on for such reflection? Recall stories of dying in which you have been so deeply involved that they have shaped your understanding of death in some significant way. Was the person who died a model for you on how effectively to cope with dying? How would you wish your dying to be the same or different? Either now or at a later time write an account of your own dying, trusting your imagination to lead you in the right direction. The writing will be richer if preceded by an imaginative experience of this anticipated event. Examine the story for the frame of reference that gives it meaning. Is the story one of hope or despair? How does it give meaning to your present existence?

It is through such reflection that we can be more aware of how we frame our stories of illness and healing. For the most part, people engage in such reflection only when they become ill. That is certainly the most likely occasion for it, and practitioners of both physical and spiritual healing should be prepared to facilitate such reflection. But how much better if people would be encouraged to engage in such reflection while they are well. That is a ministry that the church is in a unique position to provide.

4

THE USE OF IMAGERY
IN HEALING

Scientific evidence that mind-body communication is a key factor in both the cause and cure of illness accounts for the greater tolerance in medicine of methods of healing that a few years ago would have been denounced as quackery. The use of the imagination to facilitate healing is perhaps the best example of this greater tolerance. This will come as no surprise to those who are aware of the medical uses of such techniques as biofeedback, clinical hypnosis, and guided imagery. Each of these works by influencing the imagination, which in turn affects physiological processes, for example, body temperature and immune function. This opens up a whole new world of healing about which we know very little. Guided imagery, which I regard as the most promising of these techniques, has unfortunately been discredited by practitioners who make excessive claims about its effectiveness. To sort out the truth claims about the healing potential of guided imagery, we will evaluate its secular uses in this chapter; in the following chapter we will examine its religious uses.

Beyond exploring the secular uses of imagery for healing, my goal in this chapter is to identify the faith factor implicit in such use. In pursuing this goal, it will be essential to keep in mind a basic distinction between the technique of imagery, which is value-free, and its faith-laden content and context. The content of healing imagery, particularly what I call the deep structure of the imagery, will be replete with images of faith in self-healing (e.g., the healer within), Eastern religion (e.g., the unity of all things), some other faith tradition (e.g., Christianity), or an eclectic hodgepodge of beliefs (New Age). The context for healing imagery, *where* it is done and by *whom*, will also be suggestive of a faith factor; a priest or pastor doing imagery in a church will evoke different images of faith than a doctor doing imagery in a hospital.

How the Imagination Works

It is the creative use of our imagination that undergirds the practice of guided imagery. Most of us associate the use of the imagination with flights of fantasy that have little to do with the real world; we can know about the real world only through the scientific method. If that is true generally for us in the West, it is even more true in the medical community, where there has traditionally been a profound distrust of any method of healing that relies on the imagination. The imagination deals with fantasy, daydreams, and the romanticism of artists and poets—appropriate in the humanities, but not in the world of medical science.

We use our imagination much more than we normally realize. Without the imagination there would be no sense of the future; we would be unable to anticipate what might be harmful or beneficial and choose accordingly. Sometimes we can direct the imagination, for instance, in planning. Sometimes it functions spontaneously, as in dreaming or waking up to find that a problem has been solved. But whether we are conscious of its function or not, the imagination is always at work influencing what we think and do. For example, the imagination puts things together in new and different ways. There would be no new hypotheses in science without it. Not only is the imagination critical for reflecting on the possibilities of the future, but it is equally important when we revisit the past. A whiff of boiling tar, the smell of burning leaves, or a song from earlier days gives vividness and intensity to our memories of that time.

The word imagination contains within it the word image, meaning a mental picture, although images can be auditory, kinesthetic, or olfactory as well. Where do images come from? Most commentators assume that images originate in the unconscious mind and bubble up to consciousness in the form of novel ideas, illuminations, or flashes of insight. As a result, they often seem to come automatically from somewhere outside oneself. J. R. Tolkien believed that the stories he wrote were more discoveries than inventions, that they arose in his mind as "given" things. Amy Lowell described poems that sprang up as spontaneous auditory images which she wrote down, and musicians have said the same about their musical compositions.

The imagination does not respond well to outside pressure or willful demand. It functions much more vividly and spontaneously in a natural state of relaxation. Most of the waking day our attention is focused on what is going on outside of us: tasks to be done, problems to be solved, places to go. In a relaxed state our minds are temporarily empty of tensions, plans, worries, and duties. At such times the mind can be receptive to what is bubbling up from underneath—slowly at first, like coffee beginning to percolate, but then more and more images begin to surface in a stream of consciousness.

The religious imagination works in a similar manner. Faith creates the images by which it lives. Faith begins with an experience of being in relation to God, such as being protected or guided in some special way. Images of faith give concrete and vivid expression to the experience of being protected or guided. Concepts such as "guardian" or "guide" are higher level abstractions of what is embodied in the image of shepherd. At the highest level of abstraction the conceptual meanings are organized into the doctrine of the providence of God. This schema gives a certain priority to images in the "knowing" aspect of faith. It is the images which are closest to our felt sense of things and express most vividly our experience at this primal level.

Images and metaphors work much better in prayer and meditation than do concepts, which do not touch the most profound part of our being and can even distort the deepest expressions of our faith. Creeds and doctrines are highly conceptual and good for "keeping the faith," but for nurturing and strengthening faith images are much more important than concepts. That is why the Bible is so full of them. Read the psalms. Better yet, read the parables of Jesus. If you have been brought up on nothing but the literal meaning of straight doctrine, you will find them almost impossible to follow.

Though I have stressed positive uses of the imagination, because of our cultural bias against imagination and because I will be arguing for the positive use of imagery in healing, we need to be aware of its destructive potential as well. It is the imagination which feeds our worries and heightens the stress that can be a source of illness. And not all forms of imagery are equally valid as healing techniques. I will be strongly critical of New Age healing practices, although it is the content rather than the technique of imagery that I will focus on. However, my warnings against images that are highly subjective or distorted should not cloud the more basic assertion that faith cannot function without the images spawned by the imagination, images which are a powerful resource for healing.

How Imagery Works

"What is the worst thing that could possibly happen?" is a question often asked by counselors to put into perspective the worries that people have about the future. Worry is the most common form of imagery for most people, and the most injurious to their health. People who worry react more to imagined consequences than to actual probabilities. The more vivid the imagination, the more destructive the images of what might happen. Worry is negative imagery at its worst, attacking people at the physical, psychological, and spiritual levels of their well-being.

What is imagery and how does it work? Most people know the answer to that intuitively, but for a long time psychology, under the influence of behaviorism, said that intuitions do not count. Why? Because we cannot, in the ordinary sense of the terms, touch, hear, smell, or see images. Imagery is a function of deeper-than-intellectual consciousness. Essentially the same cognitive processes are used as when we are seeing or hearing something, the only difference being that the external stimulus is absent. You can test that by imagining that your hand is in a bucket of ice-cold water. If you have a vivid imagination, your hand will become colder, because your body is responding as if it were an actual sensory experience. Images of self and world can become so powerful and fixated that perceptions are forced to fit them, as is often the case with anorexia nervosa patients who are convinced that they are overweight. The internal image of being overweight is stronger than the external image reflected in the mirror.

Most people (about 95 percent) can form a visual image in full wakefulness when given a specific instruction, though the vividness and quality of the image will vary greatly. In one study 97 percent of subjects could form visual images, 59 percent could form auditory images, and 39 percent could form an image of smell. Ninety-six percent of adults report at least some daydreaming activity every day, mostly in the form of visual images of people, objects, or events. Persons who are 18 to 29 years of age report more frequent daydreams than those between 30 and 39, while persons from 40 to 49 report the fewest number of daydreams of the three age subgroups studied.

Vividness and control are the chief variables in imagery formation. High vividness and good control are the best combination for effective imaging. Low vividness and low control are characteristic of people who say they cannot do imagery or are not interested in it. Vivid imagers have fuller and richer memories than others have. They recall events by reliving them and experiencing the events as if they were happening in the present. Vividness can be enhanced through relaxation, concentration, and practice. Having a trusted guide enhances vividness and assures control, and doing imagery in a group will cause most people to be much more confident about their ability to do imagery.

Essential to everything that follows is the assumption that there is a connection between imagery and bodily function. That is so well demonstrated by studies that it is no longer a matter of controversy. Herbert Benson cites an example of the effect of image on somatic response with which most of us can easily identify: "When the film *Lawrence of Arabia*, the desert classic starring Peter O'Toole, came out a number of years ago, there were reports that concession stands were inundated at intermissions with demands for drinks—despite the fact that many of the theaters were air-conditioned or in cool climates. A veritable epidemic of thirst hit many moviegoers as they became immersed in the hot, sandy story they were viewing on the screen."[1]

How Guided Imagery Works

Guided imagery is a technique for facilitating the use of the imagination for a therapeutic or religious purpose. A state of relaxation is induced that has the effect of transporting the person to an interior place, perhaps with a room furnished in any way that the imagination suggests. Once inside the inner world of awareness, a person who has the capacity for interior reflection is ready for a free flow of the imagination that can be either quite spontaneous (images flowing from the unconscious) or structured (images suggested by a guide). Actually, both forms can be guided, but the guide has a different function in each.

A guide who is using imagery in therapy will generally encourage his or her client to be receptive to whatever images may emerge from the unconscious. A guide is needed because the images that surface are likely to be conflictual and/or highly emotional. In the structured form of guided imagery, images are suggested by the leader of the exercise. They may be images of faith drawn from a particular story, such as a healing story of Jesus, or from a storehouse of images that are shared by many people, such as the image of Jesus, the Good Shepherd. What distinguishes this type of imagery from the more unstructured variety is the control exercised by the leader. The experience is less subjective, further removed from unconscious material, and thus likely to be less conflictual and emotional. Structured guided imagery lends itself well to use within groups. It is both

1. Benson, *Beyond the Relaxation Response*, p. 3.

safe and nonintrusive, and it is usually enhanced by the presence of others who are engaged in the same activity.

Guided imagery can be done effectively only by methods that access the right hemisphere of the brain. The left brain specializes in analytic, logical thinking, especially in verbal and mathematical functions. Its mode of operation is primarily linear, processing information sequentially. The right brain specializes in synthesis, integrating many inputs at once into patterns and wholes. Imagery is a function of the right brain, as is the processing of emotions and making judgments. As such, imagery has access to autonomic functions of the body in a way that verbal commands do not. You can consciously tell yourself to raise your hand but not your blood pressure. For that you must use imagery such as a bear crashing through the bush directly in front of you. That *will* raise your blood pressure and do so by communicating directly with your autonomic nervous system via the right brain.

Perhaps the strongest evidence that visualization is a right-brain function comes from split-brain patients who have had nerve fibers severed between the two halves of their brain in order to control severe seizures. Patients undergoing this procedure report dreaming stops immediately following the injury and also note a deterioration of imagery in the waking state. It is assumed that imagery is still being formed, but the split-brain patient is unable to report it due to lack of communication between the right and left hemispheres.

It should also be noted that the portion of the brain that produces imagery is abundantly interconnected with the limbic system, the processing area for emotions, as well as with the hypothalamus and pituitary gland, both critical in the maintenance and regulation of body function and in immuno-competence. The neuroanatomic bridge between imagery and physiology is of crucial importance in understanding both the onset of illness and healing modalities that are related to the imagination.

There are different levels of imagery. Physical imagery is the most common form used in medicine, made famous by the Simontons in cancer treatment. The patient is asked to generate images that are either replications of physical features, such as white blood cells, or symbols of the same. Physical imagery as such has no faith element in it, though there will always be an implicit belief system in the imagery or in the person who uses it. Focusing on what I call the deep structure of healing imagery makes this belief system explicit. Too little attention is paid to the deep structure of physical imagery, and not many people who use physical imagery are even aware of its presence. It is when people sense a conflict between the deep structure of the physical imagery and their own belief system that the significance of the deep structure becomes apparent. For example, Bernie Segal notes that the Simonton brand of physical imagery is not for everyone:

> Since their initial patients were an aggressive group, they assumed that everyone would be comfortable attacking and killing cancer. A majority of people are profoundly disturbed by any picture of themselves killing anything, even an invading disease organism. The prevailing medical imagery of warfare is terribly upsetting to such people, even if they aren't conscious of it. Medical jargon words like *assault, insult, blast, poison,* and *kill* cause conscious and unconscious rejection by the patient.[2]

It is the deep structure of imagery that is of particular importance for our purposes, and we will examine it further in a later section on identifying the faith factor in the use of imagery.

The Use of Imagery in Medicine

As noted earlier, modern medicine has regarded consciousness of either perceptual or imaginal events as a mere "epiphenomenon," having no causal effect on physiology. That attitude remains much the same today in orthodox medical circles in relation to organic disease, though there is an increasing use of imagery for control of pain, as a method of relaxation, and as a method of treating psychosomatic ailments. In the reform move-

2. Bernie Segal, *Love, Medicine, and Miracles* (New York: Harper & Row, 1988), p. 155.

ments, such as behavioral and holistic medicine, imagery is seen as psychotechnology which holds great promise as a therapeutic tool.

Images can either precede or result from physiological changes, can be induced by conscious intention or passively received from the unconscious, and can influence the function of the autonomic (involuntary) nervous system. Because imagery originates in the right hemisphere of the brain, which is also the source of emotional responses, it serves as a vital link between consciousness and the internal working of our bodies. Imagery associated with stress may elicit inappropriate fight or flight responses in the body, and imagery associated with feelings of helplessness and hopelessness may depress the immune system and in extreme cases shut the body down completely. On the other hand, imagery that induces relaxation and expectant trust can facilitate healing and reinforce the body's natural defenses.

Though we know that imagery contributes in these ways to both illness and wellness, what we don't know is (1) how much a factor imagery is in both the cause of illness and the process of healing and (2) the degree to which we can intentionally use imagery for healing and maintaining wellness. Those questions can be answered only through carefully controlled research studies, and thus far there are very few of them.

Imagery is used in a variety of ways in the health care field. It is a part of all health care in that every diagnosis and treatment creates some kind of image in the patient's mind, sometimes far from the reality, as Susan Sontag reminds us. The most widely accepted use of imagery in medicine is for relaxation. It is commonly used for slowing down the heart rate, lowering blood pressure, and generally achieving a homeostatic balance. As a key ingredient in biofeedback, imagery is used to control autonomic functions such as body temperature. Imagery can also be used as a diagnostic tool in that images express body wisdom. Its most valuable use, at least potentially, is in the treatment of illness, though there is considerable controversy about the types of illness for which imagery is considered appropriate. Symptom control (e.g., of pain) is generally accepted, but for most physicians treatment of organic disease is not. Finally, imagery is used to rehearse anxiety-provoking events such as natural childbirth and the painful treatment for burns.

The Use of Imagery in Cancer Therapy

The bulk of the research on the use of imagery in healing has examined the effect of imagery on the immune system. The known effects of imagery are both destructive (depressed immunity in those feeling depressed) and constructive (enhanced immunity in those who cope well). However, the evidence from research is far from conclusive at this point, and considerable controversy surrounds the question of whether imagery should be used for the prevention and cure of illness. There is relatively little controversy about prevention, for example, relaxation imagery for control of stress. The real bone of contention is in the use of imagery for the cure of organic disease, particularly cancer.

The most celebrated example of using imagery in healing is the program of cancer treatment that was initiated at the Cancer Counseling and Research Center in Dallas under the direction of Carl and Stephanie Simonton. They received wide media attention after they published reports of increased longevity and decreased morbidity in their best-selling *Getting Well Again*.[3] Their work continues to receive both high praise and strong criticism. The Simontons based their research and treatment on the surveillance theory of cancer, which assumes that scattered malignant cells are likely to be present in healthy people but held in check by their immune system. It is only when the T-cells of the immune system fail to recognize or eliminate them that cancer cells are able to multiply into a full-grown cancer.

Research was done at the Simonton Center on exceptional survivors of Stage IV, widely metastatic cancer. Life expectancy for this group on the national average was one year or less. A profile of those patients who lived longer than expected was generated

3. O. Carl Simonton, et al., *Getting Well Again*.

from a number of psychological tests and compared with profiles of patients who succumbed within the time predicted.

> The patients who outlived their expectancy were more creative, more receptive to new ideas, flexible, and argumentative. Often they were downright ornery. They had strong egos and expressed feelings of personal adequacy and vitality. Rather than seeking some outside source of emotional strength, they turned to their own inner resources. They sought out innovative medical treatment, refusing to accept the death sentence handed out with their diagnosis. In this sense, they were seen as using a form of denial—not denying the seriousness of their disease by any means, but denying that they would be the victims.[4]

The treatment that these patients received was designed to reinforce the medical treatment they were receiving. The use of imagery was a key ingredient in the treatment. Patients were asked to draw pictures of their cancer and also of the treatment that they were receiving. They were then trained in the use of imagery, which was presented as a tool which they could use to influence their immune systems. The Simontons soon discovered that the imagery patients used was closely related to their rate of survival. For example, one patient who was deteriorating rapidly despite the fact that he was practicing the imagery regularly, described his image of the cancer as "a big, black rat." When asked how he envisioned his treatment, which was chemotherapy in the form of little yellow pills, he said that the rat occasionally ate one of the pills and got sick for a while, but then it would get better and bite him all the harder.

   The research team at the Simonton Center developed a projective test, called the "Image CA," for analyzing cancer imagery. After patients were educated about the disease process, how treatment might be working a change for the better, and how the immune system works as the body's defense, they were trained in the use of imagery so that they could imagine these processes in action. After drawing the images which emerged through this process, patients were asked by an interviewer to describe the

4. Jeanne Achterberg, *Imagery in Healing: Shamanism and Modern Medicine* (Boston: New Science Library, 1985), pp. 180f.

interaction between the cancer cells and the white blood cells of the immune system. All of these data were then scored for such factors as vividness, activity, and strength of the cancer cell, as well as the choice of symbolism and the regularity with which they image a positive outcome. Amazingly, scores predicted with 100 percent accuracy those who had either died or shown evidence of significant deterioration during a two-month period, and with 93 percent accuracy who would be in remission.

The features of symbols (size, activity, numbers, etc.) proved more effective for predicting outcome than the kind of symbols. There was a pattern to symbols chosen. Figures like the Knights of the Round Table, who were protectors of endangered people, were associated with a positive outcome. Animals with killer instincts such as sharks, bears, and mean dogs were regularly, though not always, associated with a good response. Very poor responses were associated with vague and weak symbols for the immune system such as snowflakes or clouds. Those with the worst prognosis were often not able to draw anything at all related to the immune system but had vivid images of their cancer.

Steven Locke, who has done a thorough review of PNI research and is sympathetic to the approach of the Simontons, notes three shortcomings in their work. First, he contrasts the difference in attitude between their missionary zeal and the more sober appraisal of others doing research in PNI; these researchers are also fascinated with "healing" images but at present explore them as hypothetical and in need of testing. Locke quotes Robert Ader: "It's one thing to argue about whether imagery works at all; a second issue to demonstrate that imagery in fact changes immune function; and still a third to say that those particular changes in immune function have any bearing whatsoever on the disease process for which the imagery was introduced in the first place. Don't misunderstand me. It's a perfectly legitimate hypothesis. But we're short of data to prove that."[5]

Second, Locke questions the scientific validity of studies

5. Steven Locke and Douglas Colligan, *The Healer Within: The New Medicine of Mind and Body* (New York: New American Library), p. 190.

showing that cancer patients who use imagery live twice as long as the national average. The Simontons matched their cases against general health statistics rather than against a control group of comparable persons not receiving the imagery therapy. This is the weakest form of controlled experiment. The Simontons' patients were a self-selected group: well-educated, intelligent, highly committed, and "healthy" in the sense of being good copers. They are not the kind of people who will lie down and die. Nor is it likely that depression, known to put people at risk for the progression of the disease, will be as great among these patients as in the average group of cancer patients.

Finally, by suggesting that cancer victims are at least partially responsible for the onset of the disease and have some control over its cure, there is danger of engendering false hope and strong guilt feelings. The power to cure the disease is the power to fail. There is no one to blame but oneself for not having the right attitude. Though a sense of well-being can improve when patients feel they have reestablished a degree of control through the use of a method that encourages participation in the treatment process, those who are vulnerable to self-doubt and depression may become more upset.

Those who continue to use imagery as a therapeutic tool are aware of the problem and insist that the attitude of their patients is realistic concerning their illness and the possibilities of treatment. Raising self-awareness and encouraging a sense of participation in the process may indeed elevate feelings of guilt, but that is true about anything for which one assumes some responsibility. Responsible therapists encourage easy-to-attain, low-level goals and warn against overdoing the therapy and overestimating what it can accomplish.

The Use of Imagery in Diagnosis and Treatment of Illness

Thus far we have been talking about how the mind communicates with the body via imagery. If we assume that the communication goes both ways, that the mind can receive information about subtle psychological processes from the body, then imagery can be used for *both* diagnosis and treatment. There are several ways that therapists have done this. Jeanne Achterberg, whose book *Imagery in Healing*[6] is the best theoretical overview of the subject, asks patients to draw images of the disease, the treatment, and the defenses against the disease. The disease imagery is assessed for the vividness of the image, its strength (or weakness), and its ability to persist, and the treatment imagery is assessed for vividness and effectiveness for curing. Martin Rossman, whose book *Healing Yourself*[7] is the best practical guide on the use of imagery for diagnosis and treatment, asks his patients to let an image form of a small animal or perhaps a wise person. Encouraging the animal or person to speak for the body, Rossman garners information that aids in both diagnosis and treatment.

According to Achterberg, it is the symbolic images, not the anatomically correct ones, that are better predictors of successful treatment. The imagery is still physical, since the symbols refer to physiological function, but the symbol often points to something more than its physiological referent. That something more is the deep structure of imagery, its meaning dimension, as is clear in this quote from Achterberg:

> After the diagnostic imagery is considered, the meaning of both the disease and the symbols used to describe the disease and the defenses against it can be addressed. . . . We inquire about what might have caused life to lose meaning, what situations were encountered that stressed a person beyond his/her limits . . . , and look for an interpretation of the problems within the patient's spiritual system of belief.[8]

Achterberg is suggesting that diagnostic imagery has a deeper structure to it, a meaning dimension made explicit in its interpretation. She makes the same point about therapeutic imagery and what it reveals about the meaning of the disease from a patient's

6. Achterberg, *Imagery in Healing*, p. 105.
7. Martin Rossman, *Healing Yourself: A Step-by-Step Program for Better Health through Imagery* (New York: Walker & Co., 1987).
8. Achterberg, *Imagery in Healing*, p. 106.

perspective. Achterberg appropriately limits herself to providing suggestions for therapists in interpreting physical imagery: keeping the images consonant with the facts, educating the person about the disease and its treatment, and creating an imaginary situation where the disease is released through both treatment and natural mechanisms. Though she is aware of the faith dimension of imagery, she offers no commentary on its content or on the context in which it is done.

I have limited my commentary to only one context for using imagery to diagnose and treat disease, the context of holistic medicine. There are others, as we will note later, but I believe the medical context to be the most responsible. To my knowledge, all those who use imagery within this context are aware that treating physical disease through mental imagery is, at best, a very slow process. If it takes ten to twenty years of stress and negative imagery to have a noticeable effect on one's health, then imagery that facilitates healing should not be expected to work any faster. Though I think the evidence that physical imagery can be a helpful resource for facilitating healing is convincing, it would be a mistake to overestimate its value. Indeed, those who so desperately turn to it as a last resort are those most likely to be disappointed. There simply is not enough time to reverse a process so deeply entrenched in the organism.

In addition, I would argue for something more than physical imagery, for example, white blood cells killing cancer cells. Such imagery fails to deal with underlying emotions. If your emotional state is one of helplessness, the physical imagery will correspond with that sense. Much of the imagery used in treatment programs attempts to reverse the negative feelings associated with an illness such as cancer by evoking a positive attitude that anticipates healing. This approach, based on the power of positive thinking, has always struck me as superficial and often dishonest in that the negative feelings are suppressed rather than changed. Much more promising is interpersonal-communal imagery that enhances awareness of a supporting network, so vitally important to those who are experiencing the isolation that almost always accompanies serious illness. For example, imagery that enhances a sense of trust in the power and presence of God has more healing potential, both physically and spiritually, than imagery that undergirds the power of positive thinking. For reasons that I will state later, it is the deep structure of imagery, suffused with symbols and metaphors of faith, that can best provide interpersonal-communal support and enhance a sense of coherence.

How Imagery Facilitates Healing

We have already noted that research supporting the use of imagery in healing is promising but not conclusive, especially in relation to organic disease. Though the evidence may seem thin to those who need hard scientific data, we are not lacking in stories about the healing power of imagery, many of which are compelling. I will limit my examples to unimpeachable sources in the medical community, people who are well known through their research and writing and are not strong personal advocates of the use of imagery in medicine. The first account comes from Eric Cassel, highly regarded medical author:

> Many years ago, while in residency training at Bellevue Hospital in New York City, I had a midnight call from the psychiatric ward: an old woman was having difficulty breathing. I found the patient gasping for air, her skin blue from lack of oxygen; she had full-blown pulmonary edema (water in the lungs) resulting from a blood clot in her lung. I sent the nurse for the urgently needed oxygen and drugs, but in those days, because of staff shortages and inexorably slow or inoperative elevators, a critically ill patient on a psychiatric ward in Bellevue at midnight might just as well have been in the East River: the wait for the necessary equipment would be interminable. I stood at the bedside feeling impotent, but the old woman's face and her distress pleaded for help. So I began to talk calmly but incessantly, telling her why she had tightness in her chest and explaining how the water would slowly recede from her lungs, after which her breathing would begin to ease bit by bit and she would gradually feel much better. To my utter amazement that is precisely what happened. Not only did her fear subside (which would not have surprised me) but the noises in her chest disappeared under my stethoscope, giving objective evidence that the pulmonary edema was, in fact subsid-

ing. By the time the equipment came, things were already under control and the patient and I felt as though together we had licked the devil.[9]

In the introduction to Norman Cousins' book, *The Healing Heart*, Bernard Lown writes of his experience as a physician specializing in cardiology. He describes a critically ill patient whose cardiac muscle was irreparably damaged and for whom all therapeutic means had been exhausted. During rounds, Lown told the attending staff that the patient had "a wholesome gallop," which indicates significant pathology of a failing heart. Several months later the patient came for a check-up in a remarkable state of recovery. He told Dr. Lown that he knew why he was better and exactly when he knew. "Thursday morning, when you entered with your troops, something happened that changed everything. You listened to my heart; you seemed pleased by the findings and announced to all those standing about my bed that I had a 'wholesome gallop.'" The image of a horse that could still go at full speed suggested to him that he could not be dying.

A third example comes from a case of imagery research. The levels of the hormone thymosin in the blood of a sixty-six-year-old man with cancer were being monitored. Thymosin is known to augment the immune response, and its concentrations provide one indicator of the potency of the immune system. Levels were checked against the man's moods and attitudes recorded in his diary. On days when he felt that the imagery was going well, the man's thymosin levels were high. On days when his diary showed that he was not participating fully in the imaging, his thymosin levels were lower. In the midst of the study, the man's wife died and he lost interest in the experiment. A blood sample was drawn at the same time, showing that his thymosin levels were noticeably depressed. The man stopped doing the imagery work; two months later, he died.

It appears from this and other examples that imagery does have healing power or at least staying potential for some people. But even that does not tell us what kind of imagery is likely to be

9. Cassell, *The Healer's Art*, pp. 13f.

helpful, only that emotions triggered by imagery can produce subtle alterations in the internal milieu, the extent and effect of which are not known. At best, imagery is one arrow in the quiver of resources available for the diagnosis and treatment of illness. There are those outside the context of responsible health care who would regard it as the primary and even exclusive method of healing. Acknowledging it as a factor in healing while admitting that no way has been found to measure its full impact leaves the door open for its continued use as a therapeutic technique and for continued research on its effectiveness.

Advocates of imagery are quick to point out that it is nonintrusive and not likely to have negative side effects other than disappointment for those who overestimate its potential. This argument is persuasive in an age that has seen a dramatic increase in iatrogenic illnesses that are an inevitable by-product of advanced medical technology. The expectant trust that people have had toward medical treatment is fading. More and more people are looking for holistic treatments that invite their active participation in the healing process. The use of imagery will continue to be a significant resource for such people, and their numbers will grow as continued research in this area provides clearer evidence concerning its effectiveness.

Identifying the Faith Factor in the Use of Imagery

Imagery is never value-free. Our task in the remaining portion of this chapter is to identify the faith factor in both the content of particular forms of imagery and the context in which they are being used. The faith factor may be explicit, but much of the time it is implicit, especially when the primary focus is on physical imagery. Though I have concentrated on physical imagery used in conjunction with medical treatment, most of the imagery used in healing is psychic and/or religious. In these instances the faith factor is usually explicit.

There is an easily identifiable faith factor in the healing imagery of shamanism, New Age healing, and self-healing. We will consider each one, but the imagery used in New Age healing will receive the closest scrutiny because the harsh criticism it has received from conservative Christianity has been unfairly generalized to include any use of religious imagery for healing. This is most unfortunate, and I will show that it results from the failure to distinguish clearly between the technique of imagery and its content/context.

The Faith Factor in Shamanic Healing

No discussion of the religious use of imagery for healing would be complete without reference to the role of the shaman, called by Jeanne Achterberg the "master of the imaginary realms." Shamanism is the oldest and most widespread method of healing with the imagination. Shamans are persons who by nature and by training are capable of altered states of consciousness in which they consult with spirit guides from whom power and knowledge for healing is obtained.

Though shamanic functions differ from culture to culture, the shaman can be described in general terms as a spiritual healer concerned about the destiny of the soul; physical healing may occur, but it is a secondary concern. It is the lost soul that is the shaman's primary concern. He searches for it, captures it, and returns it to its rightful body, thus restoring harmony to the person who is ill and to the entire community which suffers through the person's illness. Health is being in harmony with the universe and all its inhabitants.

With the aid of rituals (drums, monotonous chants, fasting, and sleeplessness) shamans are able to enter at will into an altered state of consciousness where vivid imagery experiences are possible. What we would call a paranormal experience is as real to them as our ordinary waking state. To accuse the shaman of deception for "pretending" to be a power animal while dancing in the animal's skin or for sucking a bloody object out of an ailing person's chest is a failure to appreciate the shaman's use of symbols to communicate from one realm of reality to another.

Although shamanic healing occurs in a wide variety of cultures and historical eras, its methods of diagnosis and healing are surprisingly similar. The shaman attempts to reestablish in the patient a sense of connectedness with the universe by entering into and closely identifying with the wounded soul of the person who is ill. The term "wounded healer," which Henri Nouwen has made popular in Christian circles, was originally ascribed to the shaman in the vast literature on this most universal and widely practiced form of healing in the history of the world.

Though Christians are not likely to encounter shamanism in its classic form, there are forms of psychic healing in our culture which are very similar to it. One example is the technique used by Lawrence Leshan, who trained himself to be a psychic healer by using meditation as a means of achieving a state in which he perceived himself and the person to be healed as one entity. The healer does not "do anything" to the person being healed other than uniting with him in the psychic realm. According to Leshan, this explains the power of prayer and the success of Christian Science. Healing is accomplished by properly locating the person in the universe, and one can do that by reaching clairvoyant reality through an altered state of consciousness. At this level All is One, and focusing intently on the fabric of an integrated universe can bring about change. As Leshan describes it in relation to one particular healing: "He was back home in the universe; he was no longer 'cut off.' . . . He was completely enfolded and included in the cosmos with his 'being,' his 'uniqueness,' his individuality enhanced."[10]

The religious dimension of shamanic healing is evident in the person of the shaman who is able to transcend the ordinary structures of the world in which we live and provide a connection between the harmonic powers of the universe and the person who is in need of healing. Both the faith of the shaman and the person who is ill are important in the healing ritual. Many, many stories of shamanic healing, often told by medical missionaries, testify to the effectiveness of this form of healing, whatever one may think of its validity. I see no reason to dispute those stories and many reasons for respecting this ancient

10. Lawrence Leshan, *The Medium, the Mystic, and the Physicist* (New York: Ballantine Books, 1975), p. 108.

method of healing. What I do find objectionable are the many sham replications of shamanic healing that one finds in workshops. Apart from a few significant exceptions, those who conduct these workshops know relatively little about shamanism and share none of its sacred history, of which one can become a part only by being deeply immersed both psychically and spiritually in the culture which produced it.

The Faith Factor in New Age Healing

The best known use of imagery for healing is its practice by those who are loosely linked to what has been called the New Age Movement. In churches where I field-tested exercises in guided healing imagery, I found it necessary on a regular basis to distinguish what I was doing from New Age attitudes and practices. While that may have something to do with the fact that these churches were located in the San Francisco Bay area, New Age thinking has spread far beyond the borders of California. Marilyn Ferguson may have been overly optimistic in her hope that what she called "the Aquarian conspiracy" would result in the initiation of a paradigm shift in Western consciousness, but she was certainly correct in stating that the New Age Movement has had a powerful appeal to people (especially young adults) whose souls are yearning for deeper levels of spirituality than they have been able to find in our culture, including its religious institutions. Since the use of imagery for healing has been so prominent in this movement, it will be useful to analyze the faith factor that underlies its usage and contrast it with what I am proposing.

There is an almost infinite variety of charismatic leaders and organizations (mostly small) in the New Age Movement who use imagery as a primary resource for healing. Though there is no single belief system to which they all adhere or organization to which they all belong, there are some common characteristics of New Age thinking which can help us to identify the faith factor in their use of imagery for healing.

The principle that all things in the universe are united appears in every expression of New Age thinking with which I am familiar. Borrowed from the religions of the East, the monistic principle is used to undergird the strong emphasis on holistic health care in the New Age Movement and is evident also in imagery exercises for healing. Health is harmony; illness is division and disruption. The value of imagery is that it induces a transformation of consciousness into a realm of being in which healing can occur in the experience of oneness. The healing imagery of the New Age Movement is full of implicit and explicit references to this universal energy, or life force (called "chi," "ki," or "prana"), which flows through us and unites us. The light of the sun is a common symbol for this universal energy, as are air and mind. The faith factor is clear and explicit. What heals is the universal energy symbolized as light or life force. Imagery facilitates its release within the person who is ill.

In this kind of exercise a person is instructed to visualize him- or herself as surrounded by white or golden light, perhaps from the sun, which enters the body with its life-giving power. This light is imaged as dazzling and unearthly. As one merges with this brilliant light, the body is transformed and seems to be more a body of light than of flesh. Every cell of the body is bathed and cleansed in the healing and balancing power of this restorative light. The person is then told to see that light becoming more and more concentrated in the area that is ill. The healing light engulfs any diseased cells, overwhelming and dissolving them. The light is overflowing with the unlimited energy of life, and the goal of the exercise is to experience its healing power.

The expectant trust which this imagery fosters is not directed toward a personal God but toward an impersonal energy. This is the chief difference between the content of Christian imagery and the imagery used by New Age advocates. The dominant image of healing for Christians is Christ the healer, and that must of necessity pervade the imagery used by Christians. That might be done in an exercise that invites participants to enter experientially into one of the healing stories of Jesus or to imagine Christ the healer as our contemporary. Either way it is the person of Christ who is the embodiment of God's love and compassion for those who are sick. Merging into the impersonal unity of the "one" is the goal of New Age imagery and the hope for healing. Experiencing the power and presence of Christ the healer is the goal of Christian imagery.

Transformation of consciousness is a value shared by all those who are part of the New Age Movement, whether their interest is in the political sphere or health care. Imagery facilitates an altered state of consciousness, which opens "the doors of perception" to achieve the spiritual healing and well-being that comes with cosmic consciousness and access to the life energy that revitalizes and unifies all things. What is a primary value to New Age proponents is perceived only as a threat by conservative Christian critics of this movement. The spiritual realm that one enters via an altered state of consciousness is satanic and poses a serious threat to the unprotected psychic sojourner. Such critics as Douglas Groothius in *Unmasking the New Age* and Constance Cumbey in *Hidden Dangers of the Rainbow* see nothing but danger in the use of imagery because, they argue, an altered state of consciousness is occult and therefore demonic. Small wonder that many Christians are hesitant even to try the use of imagery. I will make a case for the constructive use of imagery by Christians in chapter 5.

A final characteristic of New Age thinking is its unqualified optimism. In the New Age vision of the future, not only individuals but institutions will be transformed by a higher consciousness of unity and love. New Age healing imagery is characterized by an attitude of often unreasonable optimism that encourages people to believe that they can be healed when that hope is quite unrealistic. A common technique is to imagine one's ideal body/self as already healed. A great emphasis is placed on the power of positive thinking to effect change, which is an asset for healing but cruel when false hope is held out to the desperately ill. By contrast, Christians have confidence that their salvation (wholeness) is assured whether their physical or emotional malady is healed or not. The promises of God give Christians a reason to be optimistic about healing, including physical healing here and now, but the ultimate hope of Christians is the fulfillment of our individual and communal yearning for the realization of wholeness in the kingdom of God.

The faith factor in New Age healing should be obvious enough on the basis of this brief review, as well as the difference between the content of this faith and that of Christianity. It is the content of the imagery, not its form, that reveals the faith factor in the use of imagery.

The Faith Factor in Self-Healing

Descriptively, self-healing is simply a statement of fact. The body heals itself all the time, and in ways that medicine cannot even understand, much less duplicate. Used prescriptively, self-healing implies that you can exercise control over the healing process in a conscious, deliberate way, such as with the use of imagery.

The implicit faith of self-healing becomes explicit with references to "the healer within" or "the inner advisor." Martin Rossman, a physician who makes extensive use of imagery in his medical practice, provides us with a good example of this in his excellent book, *Healing Yourself*:

> When you are ready, invite your inner advisor to join you in this special place . . . just allow an image to form that represents your inner advisor, a wise, kind figure who knows you well . . . let it appear in any way that comes and accept it as it is for now . . . it may come in many forms—a wise old man or woman, a friendly animal or bird, a ball of light, a friend or relative, a religious figure. You may not have a visual image at all, but a sense of peacefulness and kindness instead. . . .

> Accept your advisor as it appears, as long as it seems wise, kind and compassionate . . . you will be able to sense its caring for you and its wisdom . . . invite it to be comfortable there with you, and ask it its name . . . accept what comes . . . when you are ready, tell it about your problem . . . ask any questions you have concerning this situation . . . take all the time you need to do this. . . .

> Now listen carefully to your advisor's response . . . as you would to a wise and respected teacher . . . you may imagine your advisor talking with you or you may simply have a direct sense of its message in some other way . . . allow it to communicate with you in whatever way seems natural. . . . If you are uncertain about the meaning of its advice or if there are other questions you want to ask, continue the conversation until you feel you have learned all you can at this time . . . ask questions, be open to the responses that come back, and consider them carefully. . . .

As you consider what your advisor has told you, imagine what your life would be like if you took the advice you have received and put it into action. ... Do you see any problems or obstacles standing in the way of doing this? ... If so, what are they, and how might you deal with them in a healthy, constructive way? ... If you need some help here, ask your advisor, who is still there with you. ... When it seems right, thank your advisor for meeting with you, and ask it to tell you the easiest, surest, method for getting back in touch with it. ... Realize that you can call another meeting with your advisor whenever you feel the need. ...[11]

Rossman makes it clear that it is not necessary to do what the advisor recommends. We can evaluate risks and benefits rationally and assume responsibility for the choice that we make. Rossman is not recommending blind faith in whatever is suggested to a person from lower levels of consciousness. Since this kind of exercise is usually done with direction from a health care provider, the person has the added protection of his or her counsel. Helping people to help themselves is a good thing, if for no other reason than that they are given some measure of participation and control in what is happening to them. Nevertheless, faith that is grounded only in oneself as healing agent is limited and ultimately idolatrous.

In an otherwise excellent manual on the use of visualization in medicine, Mike and Nancy Samuels state: "All people can have contact with the information necessary to direct their own growth and fulfillment. This information comes from a part of them deeper than their ego, a part *that works by itself*."[12] The same point of view carried to an extreme is found in a best-seller titled *Creative Visualization*. This is defined as the technique of using your imagination to create what you want in your life. The author means exactly that: a person only needs to *believe* that it is so in order to have whatever he or she wishes. How is that possible? By "connecting with your higher self, the God-like being

11. Martin Rossman, *Healing Yourself* (New York: Walker & Co., 1987), pp. 103f.

12. Mike Samuels and Nancy Samuels, *Seeing with the Mind's Eye: The History, Techniques and Uses of Visualization* (New York: Random House, 1975), p. 148.

who dwells within you. Being in contact with your higher self is characterized by a deep sense of knowingness and certainty, of power, love, and wisdom. You know that you are creating your own world and that you have infinite power to create it perfectly."[13]

As so often happens in the literature on self-healing, faith in oneself is closely linked to narcissism. Implicit also in this literature is the belief that we are personally responsible on a conscious or unconscious level for our state of well-being. An example is Louise Hay's *You Can Heal Your Life*. Among other extravagant claims, she says, "We are each 100 percent responsible for all of our experiences. . . . We create every so-called 'illness' in our body," and "when we really love ourselves, everything in our life works."[14]

These examples, though extreme, are the logical consequence of narcissistic faith linked to fantasy. That so many people purchase these books is an indication of their wide appeal. This is magical thinking, nothing more, and those who are desperately ill and in need of a miracle are the most vulnerable. In addition to fostering unrealistic expectations, it lays a burden of guilt on top of the suffering already borne by victims of illness. The logic is simple: If you have not succeeded with visualization, either you have not grasped the lesson that the illness is trying to teach you or you are spiritually weak. If you are the source of your illness and healing, then you are your own worst enemy when you are sick. This is a cruel hoax perpetrated on people who are in need of faith that supports rather than undermines realistic hope for healing.

As is clear from the above examples, faith in the "healer within" runs the gamut from consciousness-raising about the body's recuperative powers to an exalted faith that one's inner capacity to achieve healing is limited only by one's desire. The

13. Shakti Gawain, *Creative Visualization* (New York: Bantam Books, 1978), p. 39.
14. Louise Hay, *You Can Heal Your Life* (Santa Monica, Calif.: Hay House, 1987).

Christian response to this varied literature on self-healing is to affirm what is true (that we do contribute to our illnesses and our healing) while criticizing what is false (that we are able to make ourselves sick and well), all the while pointing beyond ourselves to the ultimate source of all healing. That ultimate source of healing is not the self, but the God who is revealed in Christ the healer.

5

THE USE OF IMAGERY
IN THE CHURCH'S
HEALING MINISTRY

The use of imagery by Christians is a natural outgrowth of the rich use of images in Scripture, and it is thus an appropriate tool for deepening the experience of what I have been calling the faith factor in healing. In this chapter, after defining the meaning of healing and wholeness, I will briefly review how imagery has been used in the Christian tradition of healing and why there has been such resistance to it. An examination of the faith factor in Christian healing imagery will follow, along with an argument for the use of structured exercises in guided imagery as a vital ingredient in the healing ministry of the church.

What do Christians mean by healing and wholeness? According to Martin Israel, a prominent Christian theologian, the answer to that begins and ends in the resurrection life of Christ.

> [Healing] commences on a simple individual plane, extends to involve human society, embraces all other forms of earthly life in its span, and finally takes in the whole created universe. Its paradigm is the resurrected body of Christ, at once individual to Jesus and yet at the same time communal for all creation, now raised from the corruption of death to the incorruption of eternal life. All other healing is partial and incomplete even if it restores the integrity of a part or organ of the body to efficient function once more.[1]

1. Martin Israel, *Healing as Sacrament: The Sanctification of the World* (London: Darton, Longman & Todd, 1984), p. 8.

This understanding of healing also serves as a correction to false expectations that people might have about healing in the church. Above all, it is a correction to the narcissism which so easily creeps into the church's healing ministry. The healings of Jesus were more than a restoration of a diseased part or organ of the body to proper function so that the person could lead a normal life again. They were a sign of victory over the powers of evil, a victory that would be finalized in his death on the cross. That means that healing is always more than a story about what is happening to me, and it never ends with my being healed of some particular disease. I am healed to live the risen life, the life of Christ, which may very well be a life of suffering like his. I am called to be a healed healer, to bring healing to human society, to all of life, to the whole created universe.

Healing is the first fruit of the resurrection. The resurrection symbolizes the indestructibility of the wholeness that comes with the gift of healing. So it was with Jesus when death appeared to end not only his physical life but also his vision of the created order as mended and made whole. The resurrection is the great "nevertheless" which reverses not only the apparent victory of death in the story of Jesus but also the little victories of disease and death in our stories of faith and hope. With faith and hope oriented around the resurrection and its promise of wholeness, the church can claim the gifts of healing which our Lord intends for us and also risk the dangers that accompany commitment to a life of service in the care of others. Given that definition of healing, does the imagination play a part in realizing the wholeness that God clearly intends?

Imagery in Faith Healing and
Christian Science

Intentional uses of imagery are new in Christian circles, but even a cursory review of the tradition of healing in Christianity will show an extensive use of the imagination in healing practices. The Pentecostal movement and Christian Science have the most fully developed traditions of healing in the history of Christianity. An example from each of these traditions will illustrate the prominence of the imagination in spiritual forms of healing.

The first is a description by Oral Roberts of his healing as he was praying. In his own words,

> A blinding flash of light of God swept over my face and eyes and spirit. . . . I felt the healing power of the Lord. It was like your hand striking me, like electricity going through me. It went into my lungs, went into my tongue, and all at once I could breathe. I could breathe all the way down.

He recollected feeling

> the presence of God . . . starting in at my feet. And it started coming up my legs. It was like, it was sort of like an electric current. . . . On the other hand, it was like a kind of warm liquid feeling that came up and came all the way up my lungs and when it got to my lungs, my lungs opened up. . . . I breathed, I got that *deep* breath, and I was clear.[2]

The language which Roberts uses could be used almost word-for-word in a guided imagery exercise—imagining electricity (read energy) or warm liquid going through you and opening up your breathing so that you can take the *deep* breath and breathe naturally.

The other example comes from Robert Peel, the eminent Christian Science author. He cites the testimonial of a person who was healed of a stubborn case of eczema. The story is typical of many other testimonials in Christian Science:

> I decided to discuss it with a Christian Science practitioner. He assured me that disease is a mortal belief that has never belonged to the man of God's creating. In my real being as God's idea, the image of the Spirit, I was subject solely to the irrefutable law of perfection and wholeness.[3]

2. David Harrell, *Oral Roberts: An American Life* (Bloomington: Indiana University Press, 1985), p. 7.
3. Robert Peel, *Spiritual Healing in a Scientific Age* (San Francisco: Harper & Row, 1987), pp. 156f.

The way to healing is to imagine oneself in "the image of the Spirit," and thus perfect and whole. Prayer in Christian Science, however else it may be defined, is a form of imagery that focuses on spiritual perfection and wholeness, and this is not unlike a guided imagery exercise in which a person imagines him- or herself being healed. The point is not that Pentecostal and Christian Science healing can be reduced to a form of guided imagery, but that they illustrate the importance of the imagination in spiritual healing.

Guided Imagery and Spiritual Healing

So dominant have been these two traditions that the term "faith healing" is linked to Pentecostals and "spiritual healing" to Christian Science. Any discussion of healing in Christianity must begin with this terminology.

The chief value of the term "faith healing" is the attention it focuses on faith as an important factor in healing, both the faith of the healer and the faith of the person being healed. It was not surprising to his contemporaries that Jesus was a healer; he was one among many. What was remarkable and quite unique was that he told people that their faith had made them well. The healings of Jesus were not something magical, something he simply *did* to people. They were relational, with the act of Jesus and the faith of the person two aspects of a larger whole. So also today. Faith does not make healing happen but is receptive to the power of God which is working through images of faith that are evoked by the Word of God. The term "faith" is used here in two ways, both as receiving instrument and as objective promise. In an exercise of guided imagery, images of faith convey the objective promise that a person makes his or her own by trusting the promise.

So is guided imagery a form of faith healing? Yes, in the sense just conveyed. No, in the sense of Pentecostal faith healing. The general tendency of faith healers such as Oral Roberts is to draw altogether too much attention to the role of faith in the process of healing. If the general Christian attitude toward healing is passivity, the typical Pentecostal attitude is overemphasis on the role of faith to the point that people who are not healed feel that they lack faith because they are not healed.

"Spiritual healing" also has drawbacks as a term used to differentiate a Christian ministry of healing from that of medicine. For many people spiritual healing is linked too strongly to Christian Science, where it refers exclusively to the healing of the spirit with no reference at all to the body. Christian Science is as narrow as biomedicine, one acting as if persons had no bodies and the other as if they had no souls. Both are distortions of the anthropology found in Scripture, which places physical healing and spiritual healing within the larger orbit of whole person healing, each with a unique contribution to make.

To others, spiritual healing refers to a supernatural action of God without any participation on the part of the person who is healed. The healings of Jesus are often interpreted this way, and modern faith healers claim to follow in his footsteps with dramatic miracle cures of their own. Most of the arguments against the authenticity of healing in the church are arguments against miraculous cures, as we noted in Chapter 3. Unfortunately faith healers have often given credence to these arguments by making exaggerated claims about instantaneous cures. Historian Vinson Synan has described Pentecostal theology as the product of an "instantaneous" mind-set. "It was Protestantism's 'crisis' mentality taken to its logical extreme. Not only was salvation an instantaneous experience, so was sanctification, the baptism of the Holy Spirit, healing, and the second coming of Christ. Nothing came gradually; every Christian experience was precipitous and cataclysmic."[4]

Instantaneous healing, however, is not a claim made by the vast majority of those who are supporting the renewal of healing ministry in the church. The more responsible claim is that God can and does work through the Word of God, prayer, the liturgy, and other means to facilitate healing at every level of need: bodily, emotional, spiritual, relational, and communal. There is

4. Vincent Synan, in a speech at Indiana University, May 13, 1983.

no more reason to expect that such healing will be instantaneous than there is to expect that medical intervention will be in the form of a "magic bullet" that will miraculously reverse the course of disease. Spiritual healing is best understood as a parallel course of treatment alongside the physical healing of medicine, each facilitating the natural/divine healing of body, mind, and spirit.

Though the term "spiritual healing" is colored by the beliefs of Christian Science and miracle cures, I think it is the best choice of a parallel term to "physical healing." Each of the terms is distinctive, yet within the larger orbit of whole person health care. Advances in physical healing through medical science have dominated the modern era, but we are beginning to understand how spiritual forces interplay with physical forces in healing. What we need is a worldview that allows for both a physical and a spiritual realm so intimately interrelated that an intervention at any level affects the dynamic equilibrium that provides a sense of coherence to the total organism.

If spiritual healing facilitates physical healing through body-mind communication, should it be submitted to the kind of verification procedures that are demanded by hard science? The common answer to this question is that spiritual healing does not lend itself to laboratory conditions.[5] Reports of healings come as testimonials rather than as research reports and will never be as persuasive as hard empirical data even when the testimonials are numerous and well documented. Complicating the matter even further, it is difficult to document the effect of spiritual care if the person is receiving medical treatment at the same time, as would likely be the case for anyone outside of Christian Science. Even though it might seem obvious that it was spiritual care that was the determining factor in a particular case, there is no way to

5. Robert Peel notes the reluctance on the part of Christian Science to participate in controlled experiments that would involve medical observation of the progress of cases under Christian Science treatment, e.g., twenty cases of cancer treated by Christian Science compared to twenty cases of cancer treated medically. "To introduce into the thought of the patient a suggestion that his or her turning to God is 'experimental' would, from this standpoint, alter the character of the relationship and possibly delay or jeopardize success" (*Spiritual Healing in a Scientific Age*, p. 43).

eliminate other variables in any single case. Scientists are not concerned about eliminating the variable of spiritual healing when testing the effectiveness of physical healing, an evident bias rarely noted.

Spiritual healing is as concrete and natural as physical healing, but much more complex and difficult to verify. When the nature of reality is larger than the frame of reference for measuring and interacting with it, the frame of reference must be modified and not the evidence of reality. There is a power operative in spiritual healing that is evidence of an orderly and creative intelligence. Though I am hesitant to speak of spiritual laws, there are empirical data to investigate if we can find the appropriate instruments to measure them. More to the point of our concern about the faith factor in imagery, it should be possible to measure the difference between religious and nonreligious imagery in healing. Research efforts are at the beginning stages of making such comparisons, and I will cite an example later. It is the complexity of spiritual healing and not its unreality or otherness that makes it difficult to measure.

Studies such as those suggested in the above paragraph would provide a healthy balance to the mostly negative assessments of spiritual healing by authors such as James Randi, William Nolen, and Louis Rose.[6] Their critique, noted earlier, serves a useful purpose in winnowing out the chaff among the great multitude of "healers" in our day. Though the critique is directed at the healers, what these authors say about the people who come for healing shows the great difference that exists between genuine faith and naive credulity. Faith is an open acceptance of a healing power and presence that is clearly perceived though only dimly understood. Credulity makes no use of rational, critical thinking and follows blindly the directions given by someone

6. James Randi used his prestigious MacArthur grant to write a scathing attack on fraudulent healing practices in *The Faith Healers* (New York: Prometheus, 1987). Earlier, an American surgeon, William Nolen, wrote an often-quoted study on spiritual healing entitled *Healing: A Doctor in Search of a Miracle* (New York: Random House, 1974). He had no more success than Louis Rose, a British physician, who had done a similar search and published his results in *Faith Healing* (Middlesex, Eng.: Penguin Books, 1968).

who has an aura of authority and power. Such credulity is the distorted form of expectant trust, and it is as destructive in its own way as the healer who exploits it.

The Faith Factor in
Christian Healing Imagery

Content and context are both crucial for discerning the faith factor in healing. As we noted in Chapter 2, the placebo is not "nothing"; it is faith, expectant trust. The question to ask about a placebo is trust in what or whom. The answer will reveal the content of faith. The Christian claim is that trust ought to be in the power of God to heal through medicine, through prayer, through the sacraments and the Word of God. The same is true about stories of illness and healing. It is in the content of the story that we will find the faith factor, and for Christians the stories are all about Christ the Healer in one form or another.

So also with imagery. It is never neutral, never without content. And it is in the content of imagery that we can discern the faith factor in healing, as we saw in Chapter 4 in relation to Shamanism, New Age healing, and self-healing. Christian healing imagery is filled with images of Christ the Healer and God acting to save the world. The Scriptures are a tissue of images, and Christian healing imagery simply draws on them to give content to its expressions of faith in a manner that is concrete and meaningful.

Context is also a key to discerning the faith factor in healing. The context of healing for Christians is obviously the church, understood as the community of faith. The more explicit that context is, the better. The worship center of the community is an excellent location for doing imagery because of the many symbols associated with the sacred space that we call the house of God. But it need not be there. A gathering of two or three Christians creates a context appropriate for healing ministry.

Christian context means more than place and people; it also means authorization and accountability. One of the flaws in the Pentecostal tradition is that too many of its faith healers are neither authorized by nor accountable to the church. Formal authorization or accountability are not always necessary, but both ought to be assumed. In the most general application of this principle, imagery should be used only after a group consensus has formed concerning its value, and accountability comes through the feedback received from the group. In a more formal sense, a congregation may wish to stipulate which persons are qualified to use imagery with groups or individuals.

Empirical Evidence of the Effects of Religious Imagery

The most dramatic examples of the physiological effects of religious imagery come from reports of stigmata appearing as a result of contemplation of the cross. Theodore Barber reports that there are at least fifty documented cases of individuals who so completely identified with the suffering of Christ that they bled spontaneously and developed skin alterations on their hands or feet which resembled Christ's wounds during his crucifixion. In a recent case a ten-and-a-half-year-old black girl of fundamentalist religious background read a book about Christ's crucifixion two weeks before Easter and was deeply affected emotionally. After seeing a television movie, she had a vivid dream about the crucifixion. Subsequently blood appeared on her palms, her chest, her forehead, and her right foot. This was observed by teachers and nurses as well as a physician who stated that after wiping blood from her palm, no lesions were found. The bleeding stopped after Good Friday.

A more typical example of the physiological effects of both expectant trust and religious imagery comes from a case cited by Martin Rossman. A woman who had been diagnosed with a precancerous condition of the cervix two years previously and had been warned repeatedly that she needed surgery to remove the affected areas ignored the recommendation four times. When asked why she was unnecessarily risking her life, she smiled broadly and said, "Jesus will heal me, and I don't need surgery." She was then asked how she communicated with Jesus, to which she responded, "I see him when I pray, and he talks to me just like we're talking now." Rossman suggested that she ask Jesus if he would heal her within the next six weeks. She did so and agreed to medical tests at that time for evidence that her condition was abnormal. "But it won't be," she said. "I know that now." Six weeks later her cervix looked normal on examination and her Pap smear was also normal.

Stories like these abound in the literature of Agnes Sanford, Francis McNutt, and Dennis and Matthew Linn, but they are anecdotal and subject to a variety of interpretations. The only scientific study of religious imagery of which I am aware was done by L. R. Propst. He monitored changes in the level of depression of forty-four male, mildly depressed, undergraduate students who scored moderately high on a religiosity scale. For purposes of investigating the use of religious imagery, all Christian in this study, Propst assigned each depressed religious student to one of four treatment modalities: nonreligious imagery, religious imagery, self-monitoring plus nondirective discussion, and self-monitoring only.

After a two-week baseline period of mild depression, students in the first three categories participated in two one-hour group sessions per week for a four-week period and kept daily mood cards. Students in the two imagery groups were also asked to relive their depressive episodes, describe the accompanying images, and be aware of depressive-engendering images. In session three, students in the imagery groups were given a list of coping statements and images directed toward modifying negative feelings related to self, environment, and the future. From this list they were to select statements and images to reduce their depression. Students in the religious imagery group used a list of religious images and coping statements (e.g., "I can visualize Christ going with me into that difficult situation in the future as I try to cope"). Students in the self-monitoring plus nondirective discussion group were permitted to discuss whatever they wanted with little therapist intervention. Students in the self-monitoring only category were informed that they were in a control group and asked only to fill out daily mood cards.

Findings indicated that (1) only 14 percent of the students who used religious imagery still scored in the depressed range as compared with 60 percent who used nonreligious imagery and 60 percent who did self-monitoring only; and (2) students who used religious imagery showed a greater increase in group interaction than the students in the other groups. A six-week follow-up study indicated that students who had used religious imagery continued to show a trend toward decreased depression as compared to students in the other groups.[7]

The Use of Imagery in the Nurture
of Spirituality

That more studies like the one just cited have not been done is probably due to a general lack of attention to the religious dimension of healing among those who do research and writing on health and healing. Even if such research were being done, the validity and effectiveness of Christian healing imagery is not dependent on the outcome. If you are interested in the use of imagery for healing but have some reservations, make the same hypothesis that others have made—that Christ's promise to heal is intended for this generation as well as his own—and then use imagery to deepen your awareness of that promise. There is a danger, of course, in making the promise too narrow (e.g., that I will be healed of *this* disease in *this* particular way and by *this* date), but faith in the sense of openness to the gifts of healing in whatever manner they are bestowed will be rewarded in ways that are often surprising and beyond the bounds of expectation.

The story is told of a man who came to the edge of an abyss and found not a steel bridge to cross the ravine but a tightrope. Across the rope came an acrobat pushing before him a wheelbarrow with a person in it. The man was impressed, and the acrobat asked him, "Do you think I can do it again?" Without pause, the man replied, "I'm sure you can." Pointing to the wheelbarrow,

7. L. R. Propst, "The Comparative Efficacy of Religious and Nonreligious Imagery for the Treatment of Mild Depression in Religious Individuals," *Cognitive Therapy and Research* 4:2 (1980), pp. 167–78.

the acrobat said, "Get in and I will take you across." The steel bridge is scientific evidence of healing effectiveness. The tightrope is the path of faith, trusting the promise of God.

The faith issue is not whether the promise of God to heal is true in general, but whether it is true for me. But even assuming faith that the promise is true for me, there are differences in the structure of that faith, and faith development theory is helpful in discerning those differences.[8] If it is a Stage 2 level of development, magical thinking abounds. Believe it strongly enough, and it will happen. God is like a doting parent who will satisfy your every desire in just the way you want it—and right now, no matter what. Many faith healers target people at this stage of faith development. At Stage 3, faith is conventional, accepting what the church teaches. That will vary considerably, of course, from one faith tradition to the next. At a Stage 4 level of faith development, claims of healing are submitted to the canons of reason. By Stage 5, faith deepens and becomes increasingly attuned to the mystery of God's healing presence in ways that far transcend an ability to grasp, much less measure, its effects. It is at this level of faith development that people resonate most deeply to the use of imagery in responding to the promise of healing that is at the very center of the gospel.

Even those who are at a stage of faith development at which imagery would be a valued resource find little in Western culture or most of Christianity that supports its usage. There is a deep hunger for spirituality among Christians in the West, and so little in our culture that meets this need.

Most people do not perceive the church as a place where their hunger for spirituality can be satisfied. In a 1978 Gallup poll 60 percent of churchgoers agreed with the statement, "Most churches have lost the real spiritual part of religion." Judging by the attraction of Eastern religions and New Age phenomena in this country, many people yearn for an inner religious experience. A recent study showed that the majority of respondents thought that getting to know the inner self was more important

8. For a description of faith stages, see Thomas Droege, *Faith Passages and Patterns* (Philadelphia: Fortress Press, 1983), pp. 50–63.

than a high-paying job, having a beautiful home, or belonging to a church or synagogue. People who have had near-death experiences report a remarkable deepening of their religious experience, and near unanimity of belief in God. However, the increase in spirituality is not matched by an increase in the activities of organized religion, which they often regard as far removed from their own experience of God.

What many people are looking for in religion but not finding in churches is something akin to a mystical experience. The word "mystical" derives from the Greek *mystos*, keeping silence. Within the silence there is a readiness for expanded consciousness, a whole-knowing that is richer and deeper than the more limited tools of analysis and critique that we normally use to interpret the world around us. Imagery is a mode of knowing which gives expression to the deeper level of reality that we are in touch with in this kind of experience.

Resistance to the Use of Imagery among Christians

Christians have discounted this kind of inner experience for so long that it it seems to have little or no value. One might call this a passive form of resistance that comes with lack of exposure to the use of imagery or any other means to stimulate inner religious experience. In some circles it is more than disregard, it is outright suspicion and hostility. I have already noted in Chapter 4 the harsh critique of imagery by Groothius, Cumbey, and others. What are the roots of such disregard, suspicion, and hostility?

The suspicion of mysticism in particular and interiority in general is stronger among Protestants than Catholics. This is not to say that Catholics have been unaware of the dangers of exploring the inner world. One of the best known of the mystics, St. Theresa, warned that "the imagination (the fool of the house) romps and frolics wildly where it wishes."[9] St. John of the Cross, another famous medieval mystic, said that the senses are being

9. From William Johnston, *The Still Point: Reflections on Zen and Christian Mysticism* (New York: Harper & Row, 1971), p. 69.

purged when one gets beyond the imaginative sphere. The goal of the meditative life is to move through meditation on images (the illuminative stage) to an imageless union with God (the unitive stage). However, awareness of the shadow side of the inner world did not deter the mystics from their quest for inner enlightenment or their encouragement of others to pursue the same quest.

By contrast, Protestantism generally has warned against the dangers of mysticism. A strong emphasis on justification by grace is matched by a similar emphasis on a fallen humanity that is completely alienated from God. A journey inward is a journey into the domain of sin that is ruled by Satan. Martin Luther insisted that our hope lies in a God who is *extra nos* (outside of us) but *pro nobis* (for us). Explore the uncharted and dangerous world of your inner experience only at the risk of your soul's salvation. Emphasis on an objective gospel that has validity and authority because of what God alone could do leaves little or no room for faith as experience. Luther says that faith is a gift of God and in no way an act of the person. Thus he warns against taking one's spiritual pulse all of the time or having "faith in faith." Instead, Luther urged his followers to keep their eyes focused on the promises of God. That is where hope lies.

Luther's attitude is typical of a general suspicion in Protestantism of a spirituality that is organized around inner experience, especially if it is an unmediated mystical experience of God. Word and sacrament are the means of grace, these alone, and they are external to the self and all of the ambiguities and distortions of inner experience. So extreme was Luther on this point that he refused to be persuaded by the most gospel-oriented of experiences, as this remarkable account shows:

> On Good Friday last, I being in my chamber in fervent prayer, contemplating with myself, how Christ my Saviour on the cross suffered and died for our sins, there appeared upon the wall a bright vision of our Saviour Christ, with the five wounds, steadfastly looking upon me, as if it had been Christ himself corporally. At first sight, I thought it had been some celestial revelation, but I reflected that it must needs be an illusion and juggling of the devil, for Christ appeared to us in his Word, and in a meaner and

more humble form; therefore I spake to the vision thus: Avoid thee, confounded devil: I know no other Christ than he who was crucified, and who in his Word is pictured and presented unto me. Whereupon the image vanished, clearly showing of whom it came.[10]

There are other reasons for resistance to the use of imagery than suspicion of inner subjective experience. One is pride, which can lead a person who has had such a profound experience to assume a position of superiority toward those who have not. Second, there is always the danger of pathology. Calling up images out of the deepest recesses of one's inner being is opening oneself to the worst as well as the best that is within. We may be afraid of meeting Satan in a journey within, but how about the neurotic and phobic fantasies that sometimes haunt our dreams and even our daytime behavior? However devout our intentions, our spirituality is not exempt from these forces. Finally, caution about unstructured interior reflection is in order because of the risk of distortion. Symbols of faith are generated and nurtured by the creative imagination, but so are distortions of those symbols.

Overcoming Resistance to the Use of Imagery

The reasons I have cited for resistance to the use of imagery are valid and must be addressed. Such resistance should be regarded as negative only when, like an entrenched defense mechanism, it becomes so rigid that it stifles the hunger for a spirituality that deepens the experience of faith. Is there imagery which can satisfy this hunger while avoiding the dangers that prompt resistance to it?

Drawing images directly from Scripture is a safeguard against a spirituality of healing that is either self-grounded or grounded in some promise other than that of the gospel. The value of a biblically based imagery is that it can remain faithful to Scripture while deepening the experience of those who are encountering

10. Gerhard O. Forde, "When the Old Gods Fail: Martin Luther's Critique of Mysticism," in *Sixteenth Century Essays and Studies*, vol. 3: *Piety, Politics, and Ethics*, ed. Carter Lindberg (Kirksville: Sixteenth Journal Pub., 1984), p. 15.

God through the text. I would argue that imagery should be subjected to the same scrutiny as preaching or any other form of witness to the gospel to ensure its faithfulness to the norm of Scripture. To condemn the use of imagery because the form of communication is different from the linear, logical mode of verbal discourse is to miss the purpose of reflecting on Scripture and to ignore the mode of communication that characterizes almost all of Scripture.

Images abound in the stories, parables, and metaphors of Scripture. These images can evoke and express faith much more profoundly than can doctrine. The imagery of Jesus as the good shepherd does more to strengthen faith than the most sophisticated theological argument does for the providence of God. The images of cross and empty tomb are more expressive of the gospel than a clear and coherent formulation of the doctrine of justification by grace through faith. The liturgy, with its heavy use of symbols and ritual actions, is closer to imagery than abstract confessional formulas. Preaching is enhanced by the use of images and stories that make faith come alive. The sacramental life of the church is enriched by images such as "heavenly banquet" and "body of Christ." In the same way imagery can deepen and strengthen the faith of God's people in the promise of healing.

Ira Progoff, a Jungian psychologist well known for his program of "Intensive Journalling," once told of writing in his journal: "Suppose the Nazis had burned all the Bibles in the world. What would happen? . . . Well, we'd just have to make new ones from the same place that the old ones were made." Progoff is not talking about the memory of the Christian community but symbols coming out of the collective unconscious. This will not do. For Christians word and sacrament provide the structure for the inward journey. They keep us in touch with the God of history who acts in our history through these means of grace. It is important to understand that one takes the inner journey in order to enhance word and sacrament, not to replace them.

Most of us are not likely to err on the side of moving too deeply into the inner world of our experience and there getting lost in pathologies or distortions of the true meaning of Christianity.

We are much more likely to err on the side of too much caution, too much resistance. The spirituality that has been nurtured in us through word and sacrament will serve as a reliable guide in any journey that we take into the inner world of experience. My advice is to take the plunge into deeper waters and use the feedback of fellow members in the body of Christ to help you reflect on the meaning of your experience.

The Use of Imagery in Prayer
for Healing

Illness has always been an occasion for prayer, but prayer does not always come easily. The discipline of private prayer is increasingly rare among Christians, many of whom do not know how to pray or find it exceedingly tedious. The use of imagery as a form of prayer can be like rain in a parched desert for such people.

Prayer is to be made less with the head than with the heart. Many people mistakenly equate prayer with thinking. Prayer can be as simple a matter as breathing in and out while concentrating on a single religious image or phrase. Rather than thinking or talking, prayer is more a matter of sensing, loving, and intuiting. If that is so, then imagery is a resource for prayer that needs cultivation.

Prayer is to the soul what breathing is to the body, and the two can be intimately interrelated through the use of imagery. For example, to imagine the Spirit of God "in, with, and under" the breath that one inhales enhances the awareness of the life-giving power of the Holy Spirit animating one's inner spirit. The inner spirit, in turn, becomes the healing force of nature that restores and renews the physical body. There is ample empirical evidence of healing power within the human organism, but the growing body of literature on "the healer within" grounds this power in the self rather than in God. Imaging the Spirit of God in the breath of life, of which there are many biblical examples, opens the portals of the personality to the full impact of the Holy (whole-making) Spirit.

With all of the evidence we have that the imagination does effect changes in the body, it does not seem far-fetched that God would act through this natural channel. But what about intercessory prayer? There seems to be no "natural" channel like mind-body communication through which the healing power of God can be communicated from one person to another. Some have argued that intercessory prayers for healing can be explained as a form of paranormal communication, such as telepathy, but that is not convincing to most people as a rational explanation. There is evidence, however, that intercessory prayer for healing works. I cite it not as empirical proof but as encouragement to greater openness on the part of people, like myself, who are so thoroughly conditioned by our scientific worldview.

A California cardiologist, Randy Byrd, arranged for a group of people around the country to pray daily for 192 patients in coronary care at San Francisco General Hospital.[11] This was part of a double-blind, randomized study of 393 coronary patients. The 201 patients in the control group did not receive prayers from the network, while the "prayed-for" group had from five to seven people in the country praying for them each day. The patients in the two groups were comparable in age and severity of conditions. The people doing the praying were given the name of the patient, the condition, and the diagnosis; they were asked to pray for "beneficial healing and quick recovery" of each person. The study was conducted over a ten-month period, and the results showed that the prayed-for subjects had significantly fewer complications during that time. Only three required antibiotics, compared with sixteen in the control group. Six prayed-for patients suffered pulmonary edema compared to nineteen in the control group. None of those who received prayer needed intubation, compared with twelve in the control group.

Quite apart from the question of how intercessory prayer works, the imagination can enliven and deepen intercessory prayer, as Morton Kelsey indicates in the following passage:

---

11. M. M. Beecher, "Three Cardiologists Report Prayers for Their Patients Are 'Answered,'" *Medical Tribune* (Jan. 8, 1986), pp. 3, 15.

In order to pray for others one must first of all be silent. Then in images one finds oneself before Christ, perhaps in some Biblical setting, and then sees oneself bringing the other person to that spot where Christ is healing or bringing insight or consolation. Obviously we are not trying to bring the person into *our* presence, unless we have a rather exalted idea of our own power. When we pray for people, we are trying to help them be open to finding contact with God, and the best way to do this is imaginatively to see them in contact with Christ. We can then share some of their pain or sorrow or lostness and help them carry it before the Christ. We already know Christ's love, and the most that we can do is to try to be adequate channels of imagination so that the reality of His loving, transforming power can move in and through others and bring them to new life.[12]

One of the most meaningful ways to engage in this type of intercessory prayer is in a group where the person being prayed for is present. It is comforting to know that you are being prayed for by widely scattered individuals who are all quite distant from you, but the awareness of being physically surrounded by loving people who are praying for you deepens that sense of comfort. Instead of having one person in the group speak a verbal prayer, a guided imagery exercise can provide guidance to the imagination of all those present in bringing this person into the presence of Christ. If the group is small, each person might put a hand on the head, shoulder, or back of the person being prayed for. Imagery prayers of healing for a person who is not present are also appropriate, of course. The principle in either case is to deepen the sense of involvement in prayer.

The Use of Imagery in Giving Expression to Bodily Spirituality

We have become alienated from our bodies. The higher we go in social status the more alienated we become. The myth of a society is expressed through the body. Those at the highest levels never get dirty, never sweat, never touch anyone, and rarely use

12. Morton Kelsey, *The Other Side of Silence: A Guide to Christian Meditation* (New York: Paulist Press, 1976), p. 234.

their bodies in an active way. Technology has freed most people from manual labor, including those who work in industry. The machine has become a model of life and a metaphor of body.

The traditional biomedical model reinforces that way of thinking about the body, treating the body like a machine in need of repair, diagnosing the problems objectively like a mechanic and prescribing treatment that will put the body back in working order. If we think of our bodies as machines, then it is no wonder that we are angry when they break down. It is like any other piece of property that we own: we expect good performance and feel let down if it does not work well.

The sense of alienation from our bodies is increased by a theology that depicts the body as evil and as a source of continual temptation. When St. Paul talks about the conflict between flesh and spirit, he is referring to the alienation of the whole person from the Spirit of God, but most people regard sins of the flesh as sins of the body. If the body is regarded as the primary source of temptation in one's life, then control if not subjugation is what will inform the spirituality of the body.

A Christian understanding of health and healing suggests a very different kind of spirituality of the body. Health is wholeness of body and spirit. Healing is getting in touch with the natural rhythms of the body. Women are generally closer to their bodies than men, partly because of the menstrual cycle and giving birth, and partly because their lifestyle until recently has not been as abusive to their bodies as the lifestyle of men (high stress, heavy smoking, hard driving). Women also have a clearer sense that wholeness is relatedness, being a part. It has been my experience that women find it much easier and more natural to do imagery than men. They are more in tune with their bodies and more willing to allow the body to express spontaneously the feelings that reside there. The best book I have read on the spirituality of our bodies was written by a woman,[13] and the best exercises that I have experienced on body movement and prayer have been led by women.

13. Flora S. Wuellner, *Prayer and Our Bodies* (Nashville: The Upper Room, 1987).

Flora Wuellner describes the experience of moving from the question "What is my body?" to the question "Who is my body?" The answers that came when she discovered the right question are expressions of a body-self that are possible only when the body is regarded as a full partner in dialogue: "I am the manifestation of the miracle which is you. I am the ground of your deep powers." "I am the faithful messenger and recorder of your memories, your powers, your hurts, your needs, your limits." "I am the stored wisdom and hurts of the ages and generations before you." "Far from separating you from your spiritual life, I open it to you." "You can pray with me, for me, through me. I can pray also, in my way, when you cannot."[14] These are wonderful expressions of the body-self when it is given an opportunity to speak.

Some of the physicians and psychologists who are using imagery in their practices have discovered the value of giving the body an opportunity to speak. Martin Rossman describes the process of letting a symptom of illness speak by relaxing the patient and allowing an image to surface that can represent the symptom. An imaginary conversation follows in which the symptom is asked why it is there, what it wants from the patient, and what it is trying to accomplish. This method does not replace the case history method but rather supplements it with an interpretation from an "inner advisor" who will have access to information unavailable even to the higher consciousness of the patient.

Symptoms are the voice of illness, friendly warning signals rather than messages from the enemy. Our bodies are incredibly intelligent and constantly attempting to communicate with us about impending problems and modes of self-healing. Yet people tend to ignore or play down early warning signals from their bodies as bad news that they do not have time for. Much attention has been given to "the art of listening" in interpersonal communication. We ought to be at least as willing to listen to our own bodies with respect and attentiveness.

14. Ibid., pp. 16f.

We experience both unity and separateness in relation to our bodies. The body-self functions on automatic pilot for the most part, quite independent of the conscious-self. At the same time we are aware of exercising control over what the body does—quite intentionally in decisions such as what we will do, eat, wear, etc., and in a more subintentioned way through our attitudes and expectations. The conscious-self is the body-self thinking and feeling. The body-self is the conscious-self breathing and acting. Through an imaginary dialogue with the body, we can give the body a means of self-expression through the use of the language of imagery, thus facilitating communication between the conscious-self and the body-self. The result can bring a greater sense of unity, identification, empathy, and understanding.

One ought not romanticize the benefits of listening to the body, as if that will always be a voice of wisdom or a voice that has the last word. Sometimes the symptoms that clamor for attention are sending misleading messages about what is going on in our bodies. And sometimes people are preoccupied with their bodies to the point of neurotic fixation, believing that every new pain or malfunction is a precursor of disaster. We need to be discerning about the messages we hear from our bodies, evaluating them in the light of past experience and learning to accept pain and bodily malfunction that cannot be changed. And at times the conscious-self will ignore messages from the body about even life-threatening situations in order to serve a higher purpose than self-survival. Such a choice, however, is not made in disdain for the body but as an act of full self-realization.

What we need is a spirituality of the body, and because imagery is the language of the body, it is a prime resource for giving expression to the body. Wuellner speaks about "letting the body pray." Breathing can be an act of praying if one concentrates on the deeper level of the activity, which is the sacramental dimension of breathing that heightens awareness of the presence of God both in and beyond our bodies. Inspiration is a term that comes from the image of God's breathing into us—quite literally in the description of Adam's enlivening and more figuratively in the description of those who wrote the sacred Scriptures. Every breath that we inhale is an occasion for reflection on the life of God within us.

Any bodily activity that deepens awareness of the presence of God is an act of worship, an act of prayer. The disciples recognized the risen Christ as he broke bread with them and prepared fish for them. We recognize and celebrate the presence of the risen Christ when we break bread at the Eucharist, when we pour water over those who are baptized, when we lay healing hands on the sick. And not only in such pious activities. Walking in the woods, physical exercise, mutual expressions of intimacy—all are occasions for the ritual of praying through our bodies.

Conclusion

We began this chapter with the observation that all healing in the church begins and ends in the resurrection life of Christ and that this understanding serves as a correction to a preoccupation with one's own need for healing. I come back to the same thought at the end because so much of this chapter has been focused on the healing of the person. Healing imagery is appealing to the self-serving narcissism that resides within us all. When this attitude creeps into the church as a motivation for healing prayer, the danger of misusing imagery is high: "I am in need of healing. God has the power to heal. Imagery is a ritual for gaining access to that power."

Prayer, including prayer for healing, should be in tune with what God intends for us and for the world, not what we want from God and from the world for ourselves. The Gospels do not keep us guessing about what Jesus intended for those who came to him for healing. He intended for them to be whole in body, mind, and spirit. What is easily overlooked, however, is that wholeness includes holiness. Those who are healed become healers. Those who are loved become lovers. Health, in the sense of individual wellness, is always a means to an end and never an end in itself. And once again, the Gospels do not keep us guessing about what that "end" is. As Martin Israel puts it:

The measure of a truly spiritual healing is the steady transformation of the person's character so that he ceases to live for himself alone, but gives himself ever more unreservedly to others. His vision of fulfillment is no longer limited by the desire for personal gain. Instead the desire is for all people to gain a knowledge of God, in whom alone there is eternal life. As a person is healed spiritually, so he gives healing to others that in the end the whole world may be transfigured from dross to spiritual radiance.[15]

The faith that heals is both expectant trust, receiving the gift of healing from God, and commitment, giving oneself in service to the cause of healing others and the world. I have put a heavy emphasis on expectant trust in the God of healing whom we know in the person of Jesus Christ. Yet the trust of faith must always be complemented by commitment to the way of the cross, the way of the wounded healer.

15. Israel, *Healing as Sacrament*, p. 51.

DATE DUE

MAR 1 0 2000			
JUN 1 3 2001			